STRATEGIC INVESTING

A guide to confident and successful investing

John A Schroeder

Table of Contents

Introduction

This book is to help all of those who have experienced one or more of the following:

- Losses during significant downturns in the market
- Disappointment in the performance of funds managed by a financial advisor
- Uncertainty regarding when to be fully invested
- Confusion from myriad opinions in the financial press
- Missing great opportunities that others have captured
- Being unclear about when to invest in bonds
- A lack of structured, data-driven decision processes
- Angst and frustration caused by some of the above

Now is the time for you to enter a new phase of investing, with better results, greater confidence in your decisions, and reduced emotional involvement. It is my hope that this book, which distills my 50-plus years of investment experience, will be of great value to you.

I started writing this book in early 2023, when the pain experienced by investors during the 2022 downturn remains fresh in many minds. It is generally understood that equity markets experience serious downturns very infrequently. However, there have been three stock market crashes since 2008: In 2008 following the housing crisis, in 2020 when the COVID pandemic began, and in 2022 as the Fed raised interest rates sharply. All three have been devastating for older investors, and we will discuss how strategic investors fared much better than the markets during these times.

Protecting capital and even profiting during these events requires more thought than simply watching stocks rise in a bull market.

Witnessing the pain and suffering of friends and acquaintances in 2022, as well as the struggles faced by the average investor, has motivated me to write this book. The markets were very challenging in 2022, and the impact of the financial crisis on investors and individuals was well documented in the media and news.

The first issue of the Investor Business Daily paper in 2023 begins with the following front-page article:

"The stock market is coming off a **punishing** year that brought **eye-watering losses** for investors."

A couple I have known for years had planned to retire in June of 2022, relying primarily upon the value of their individual IRA accounts. Their financial advisor had endorsed their plan. By May of 2022, after experiencing severe declines in their IRAs, they were both forced to postpone retirement. Sadly, countless other people found themselves in a similar situation.

According to an article in Barrons on January 5, 2023, "*The average IRA balance plunged 25% year over year as of the third quarter of 2022 according to Fidelity. To break even, those investments would have to rise 33%.*"

The losses people endured in 2008 were, on a percentage basis, even worse than 2022. The high was in October 2007 at 1576 on the S&P 500 Index. The low occurred in March 2009 at 667. That's a loss of 909 points, or 57.7%. Who could tolerate that?

Note: your author was not in any stocks during 2008.

Andrew W. Lo, in his book *Adaptive Markets* (2017), reflected on the severe drop caused by the housing crisis. (He does not discuss the drops in 2020 or 2022 as his book was published before either of these two events.)

"Why were we so unprepared? In part because we were told it couldn't happen that way…We should buy and hold a passive, well-diversified portfolio of stocks and bonds, or an exchange-traded fund requiring as little thought as possible" (Lo, 2007, p. 5).

This is consistent with something called the *Efficient Market Hypothesis*, popularized by Burton Malkiel in his 1973 book, *A Random Walk Down Wall Street*. Malkiel was an economist at Princeton.

According to an article by Forbes, "The Efficient Market Hypothesis argues that current stock prices reflect all existing available information, making them fairly valued as they are presently. Given these assumptions, outperforming the market by stock picking or market timing is highly unlikely, unless you are an outlier who is either very lucky or very unlucky."[1]

The phrase Buy and Hold became popular as a strategy derived from the Efficient Market Hypothesis.

The assumption that market timing is impossible still persists in the minds of many investment managers and was frequently expressed by them on CNBC during 2022. When asked whether they were lightening up on stock during the bear market of 2022, many said that no, "We are not market timers, so we remain fully invested."

Let's think about that for a minute. Early in 2022, the Fed Open Market Committee and Fed Chairman Jerome Powell made it clear that, due to the significant rise in inflation, the Fed would

---

[1] reference: https://www.forbes.com/advisor/investing/efficient-market-hypothesis/

implement a series of interest rate increases throughout 2022, which would measurably slow the economy. So, in light of that, did it make sense to remain fully invested and just suffer the painful losses? Certainly not, yet many money managers did just that.

Morgan Stanley, a well-managed investment bank, has many senior economists and portfolio managers. Yet in 2022, the mutual funds run by Morgan Stanley lost in some cases more than 40% of their value. How do you feel about paying a management fee for that? If you wish to confirm my statements about Morgan Stanley mutual funds, please look up a graph on Barchart.com for MPAIX, their Advantage Portfolio; MPEGX, their Discovery Portfolio; or MBVX, their American Resilience Portfolio.

The IRA accounts I manage suffered very little in 2022, and in 2021 (a strong year), they were up 28%. The decisions I make are data-driven, utilizing tools that I have developed, as well as data and tools widely available to the public. This book will prepare you for bear markets and give you the ability to outperform the indices by wide margins.

Let's recap what went wrong, making the average investor take such a bath in 2022. Here are some of the primary reasons:

1. The belief that bonds are safe when stocks are weak. While this is often true, it was the complete opposite in 2022. Bond prices and interest rates move inversely, as explained in later chapters, and the Federal Reserve Open Market Committee made it clear they would be raising rates significantly that year. It was no surprise to anyone following the Fed that bonds would decline in value.

2. Blindly following the advice of financial advisors who claim one should not try to "time" the market, rather one should stay invested in solid companies, and that the

returns will be good over time. This advice may be acceptable to an investor in their 20s or 30s, but it can cause significant problems if you are older. As we will see in Section II, there are instances when the strategic does not invest in stocks at all.

3. Making decisions based on emotion, not proven principles. It is well known that individual investors are wrong more often than right, to the extent that some use the sentiment of small investors as a contrary indicator with good results. Sad but true.

Note the following quote on the website of AAII, The American Association of Individual Investors, regarding their Sentiment Survey of individual Investors:

"The Sentiment Survey is a contrarian indicator. Above-average market returns have often followed unusually low levels of optimism, while below-average market returns have often followed unusually high levels of optimism."

The strategic investor is logic-driven and does not invest based on how he feels or what his brother-in-law is doing. His behavior is in stark contrast to that of the typical investor surveyed by AAII.[2]

Having reviewed past downturns and noting that we can often avoid most of them, as you'll see in more detail later, it is important to say that this book mainly focuses on recognizing when markets offer great opportunities to invest—sometimes in stocks, sometimes in bonds, and sometimes in real estate. We can prevent ourselves from financial and emotional hardship by steering clear of declining markets, but for most of us, our profits tend to come during bull markets or flat markets, where there are still significant opportunities. My hope in sharing my knowledge

---

[2] See https://www.aaii.com/sentimentsurvey.

is that you will become confident and profitable in nearly all market and economic conditions.

The Structure of this book

This book has 3 major sections. You will notice that a lot of the content in sections II and III is actionable. By that, I mean it presents methods and tools for your use. This isn't a book for casual reading but rather a guide to help you improve your maturity as an investor, with tangible results serving as proof of your success.

Section I Essential Concepts

This section covers topics that are critical to our discussion of strategies in sections II and III. For example, in section I, chapter 2, we discuss bond basics including duration and yield. These concepts are needed for the discussion of bond strategies in Chapter 7. The usage of Section I content in strategies is very evident in Section II.

Note: The reader may wish to go beyond what is presented in Section I for his own edification, but that should not be necessary to understand the strategic discussions in Sections II and III.

Section II Strategies

This section covers strategies for investing in equities, bonds, real estate, and cash. Yes, cash is considered an asset because asset allocation among these four classes is crucial, and there are times when having a significant cash position is wise. This part provides guidance on when and how much to invest in each major category and how to choose investment options. Timing is key, and this section offers advice on when to make investment commitments and when to exit. As you'll see, there are periods when you should avoid being long on equities. This section references Section I. For example, both technical and fundamental analysis are used in the chapter on equity strategies (chapter 5), as both should be conducted before making new commitments.

Section III Putting It All Together

This section covers strategies for investing in equities, bonds, real estate, and cash. Yes, cash is considered an asset because asset allocation is essential among these four classes, and there are times when your cash position should be significant. This section provides guidance on when and how much to invest in each major category and how to select investment candidates. You will also find important advice on risk management. Timing is crucial, and this section offers guidance on when to make investment commitments and when to exit. As you'll see, there are times when you should not be long equities! This section relies on Section I. For example, both technical and fundamental analyses are used in the chapter on equities, as both should inform new investment decisions.

As you become more structured in your investing, you will take on more of the qualities that characterize what I consider a Strategic Investor:

1. He/she is aware of Federal Reserve policies and forward guidance and can interpret what significance they have for the investor

2. He/she can recognize when to be aggressive in holding equities and when the risks require a defensive approach

3. He/she understands the fundamentals of bond pricing, the yield curve, and when risks are elevated in holding long-duration bonds.

4. He/she understands the opportunities real estate presents for long-term accumulation of equity and strategies for tax-free gains.

5. He/she continuously reassesses the allocation of assets between equities, bonds, real estate, and cash and does so based upon the state of the economy and the markets.

6. He/she can communicate at a high level with financial planners and/or investment managers.

7. He/she feels confident in making his/her own investment decisions with or without the help of investment managers.

Becoming more structured in your investment decisions has benefits that extend beyond the financial rewards. This book should not only improve your financial performance, but it will also help you sleep better and avoid regret for decisions you've made. Investing should be objective and not a continuing emotional experience. Yes, there will be investments that are not profitable, but they will be outnumbered by those that are, and you will develop confidence in your decision-making over time.

About the Author

Just the highlights; this is a book about you, not about me. Nonetheless, I need to provide you with enough information about my background so that you can decide whether to accept me as a mentor or not. You already know a little about me from the Introduction if you read between the lines. I have a high regard for clear logic and structured thinking. This is partly a product of an education in mathematics (applied math at Purdue, theoretical math at UC Berkeley). I also like to be succinct. I have many years' experience in equities, futures, and real estate investments. I was recognized as a "Top Gun" in Stocks and Commodities magazine after participating in a 6-month futures trading contest. My real estate investments intensified following the guidance from the Fed that they intended to inflate assets after the 2007 mortgage crisis, and after they realized that low interest rates were not having as positive an effect as they had anticipated. Similarly, I capitalized on the near-zero rates following the onset of COVID-19. I taught Financial Engineering in the University of California's master's program for six semesters and had waitlists for every semester following the first.

I am now largely retired, except for managing and updating the software I have written, which executes trades in S&P futures without my intervention, and managing IRA accounts for two close friends. My wife and I split our time between our homes in Colorado and Maui. My experience base is rich, and it is time for me to give back, hence this book.

Included in my experience are the early periods in my life as an investor when I committed some of the sins I would like to help you avoid. My decisions were often based on intuition rather than logic, and when losses occurred, I felt feelings of inadequacy and failure. Over time, I became increasingly data-driven and logic-oriented, which resulted in greater confidence and success.

My hope is that, with the help of this book, you will transition to becoming logic-driven and strategic more quickly than I did.

Section I
Essential Concepts

Chapter 1: The Federal Reserve System

The Federal Reserve System could be a lengthy subject for study in its own right. We need to understand the structure, functions, and processes only at a level that allows us to intelligently use the information the Fed provides to guide our views of the economy and what changes are coming to interest rates and whether the Fed is going to be accommodative to expansion or putting on the brakes to slow the economy. As we will see, the Fed is quite transparent about its views of the economy, inflation, and how it foresees changes to interest rates. An investor who follows the Fed's guidance has a huge advantage over one who does not.

1.1 Overview of the Fed and Its Functions

"Congress has entrusted the Federal Reserve with great responsibilities. Its decisions affect the well-being of every American and the strength and prosperity of our nation. That prosperity depends most, of course, on the productiveness and enterprise of the American people, but the Federal Reserve plays a role too, promoting conditions that foster maximum employment, low and stable inflation, and a safe and sound financial system."

— Chair Janet Yellen, Nov. 14, 2013

The Federal Reserve System is the central bank of the United States. It is an independent agency of the U.S. government. It does not receive funding through the congressional budgetary process. Its funds are derived primarily from interest earned on government securities that it owns. No elected official is allowed to serve as one of the members of the Board of Governors, the body that oversees the operations of the Federal Reserve System.

The following are the five purposes of the Fed. The first of these, conducting monetary policy, is the function of greatest interest to investors, as we will see throughout this chapter.

The Five Functions of the Federal Reserve:[3]

1. Conducts the nation's monetary policy to promote maximum employment and stable prices in the U.S. economy

2. Promotes the stability of the financial system and seeks to minimize and contain systemic risks through active monitoring and engagement in the U.S. and abroad;

3. Promotes the safety and soundness of individual financial institutions and monitors their impact on the financial system as a whole;

4. Foster's payment and settlement system safety and efficiency through services to the banking industry and the U.S. government that facilitate U.S.-dollar transactions and payments; and

5. Promotes consumer protection and community development through consumer-focused supervision and examination, research and analysis of emerging consumer issues and trends, community economic development activities, and the administration of consumer laws and regulations.

This book places a discussion of the Federal Reserve System in an early chapter because, when it comes to making and communicating policy affecting both short and long-term interest rates, the Fed (Federal Reserve System) is the "elephant in the room". The strategic investor pays close attention to changes in

---

[3] source: https://www.federalreserve.gov/aboutthefed/the-fed-explained.htm

monetary policy and to the Fed's forward views on the economy and its anticipated policy responses.

We will look at Fed actions and communications primarily since 2007, since their views on inflation, fed funds rates, and the use of bond purchases have matured over time and experienced some lasting changes in response to the housing crisis and recession of 2007, 2008, and 2009. We will look at a most interesting retrospective written by Ben Bernanke in 2012 on the policies and tools the Fed used during these years, and which have lasting effects on the Fed's method and strategies from that period up to the present.

1.2 The Structure of the Federal Reserve System

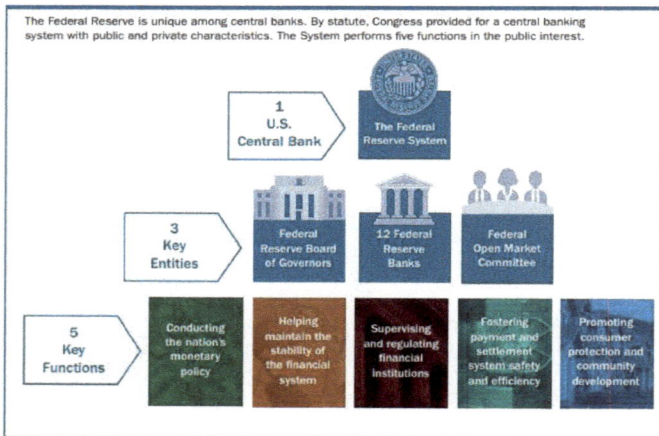

The Federal Reserve is unique among central banks. By statute, Congress provided for a central banking system with public and private characteristics. The System performs five functions in the public interest.

There are three key entities within the Federal Reserve System: the Board of Governors, the Federal Reserve Banks (also known as Reserve Banks), and the Federal Open Market Committee (FOMC). The Board of Governors, an agency of the federal government that reports to and is directly accountable to Congress (figure 1.2), provides general guidance for the System and oversees the 12 Reserve Banks.

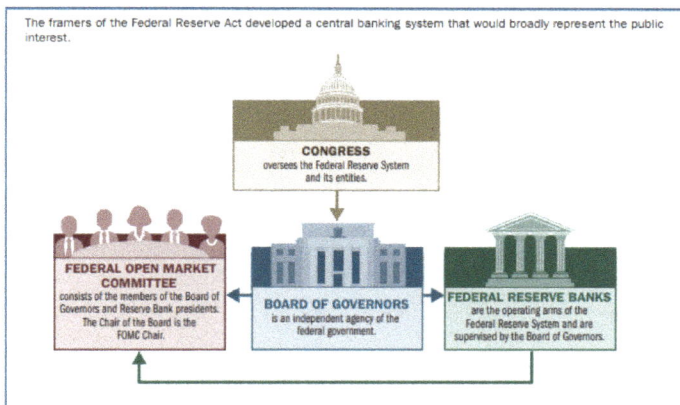

The framers of the Federal Reserve Act developed a central banking system that would broadly represent the public interest.

CONGRESS
oversees the Federal Reserve System and its entities.

FEDERAL OPEN MARKET COMMITTEE
consists of the members of the Board of Governors and Reserve Bank presidents. The Chair of the Board is the FOMC Chair.

BOARD OF GOVERNORS
is an independent agency of the federal government.

FEDERAL RESERVE BANKS
are the operating arms of the Federal Reserve System and are supervised by the Board of Governors.

1.3 Monetary Policy and Forward Guidance

For investors, the actions of the Federal Open Market Committee (FOMC) are of primary importance, and we will examine them in detail here. We will examine later in Section II examples of how investors have utilized the information provided by the FOMC to their distinct advantage. In the chapters that follow on Equities and Bonds, the results of the Fed's actions will be visible through concrete examples.[4]

"The Federal Reserve conducts the nation's monetary policy by managing the level of short-term interest rates and influencing the availability and cost of credit in the economy. Monetary policy directly affects interest rates; it indirectly affects stock prices, wealth, and currency exchange rates. Through these channels, monetary policy influences spending, investment, production, employment, and inflation in the United States. Effective monetary policy complements fiscal policy to support economic growth."

"To promote public understanding of how the Federal Reserve interprets its statutory mandate, the FOMC released its "Statement on Longer Run Goals and Monetary Policy Strategy" in January

---

[4] https://www.federalreserve.gov/aboutthefed/files/the-fed-explained.pdf#page=24

2012. This statement explains the FOMC's longer-run goals and its strategy for setting monetary policy to achieve them. In the statement, the FOMC also established a numerical longer-run goal for inflation: In the Committee's judgment, an annual rate of increase of 2 percent in the price index for personal consumption expenditures—an important price measure for consumer spending on goods and services—is most consistent, over the longer run, with meeting the Federal Reserve's statutory mandate to promote both maximum employment and price stability. The FOMC reaffirms its goals statement at its January meeting each year.[5]

Forward guidance signals the FOMC's policy Intentions. In addition to adjusting the target for the federal funds rate, the FOMC can also influence financial conditions by communicating its intentions for future policy adjustments. Since March 2009, when the federal funds rate was effectively at its lower bound, this form of communication, known as "forward guidance," has been a crucial signal to the public of the FOMC's policy intentions. For example, when the FOMC said in its March 2009 post-meeting statement that it intended to keep the target for the federal funds rate "exceptionally low" for "an extended period," its goal was to cause financial market participants to adjust their expectations to assume a longer period of lower short-term interest rates than they had previously expected and, thus, put downward pressure on long-term interest rates to provide more support for the economic recovery. Between 2009 and 2014, the FOMC revised its forward guidance several times, strengthening its intent to put downward pressure on interest rates when the economy appeared to be operating at a lower level than desirable and, more recently, revising it to clarify how, when the time was appropriate, the

---

[5] https://www.federalreserve.gov/aboutthefed/files/the-fed-explained.pdf#page=24

Committee would make the decision to raise the target federal funds rate.

1.4 FOMC Primary Communications Tools

Statements after FOMC meetings.

Since 1994, the Federal Reserve has issued statements announcing FOMC decisions. In recent years, those statements have summarized the Committee's judgment about the appropriate conduct of monetary policy over the next few quarters. The release of post-meeting communications often provides the broader context for FOMC policy decisions. The statements following the FOMC announcements also typically contain forward estimates of GDP (Gross Domestic Product) and interest rates. See the FOMC's most recent post-meeting statement at

www.federalreserve.gov/monetary policy/fomccalendars.htm.

FOMC decisions are announced on Wednesdays at 2:00 PM Eastern Time, accompanied by a statement from the Fed Chair at 2:30 PM Eastern Time. The calendar of meetings is found here:

https://www.federalreserve.gov/monetarypolicy/fomccalendars.htm

Strategic Investors listen to the Fed announcements and statements. CNBC is a good source that broadcasts the Fed Chair's summary of FOMC decisions and the Fed chairman's overview of the economy. Other financial channels broadcast the same. Listen in real time or record it for later viewing.

A) Meeting minutes

Detailed minutes of FOMC meetings are released three weeks after each meeting.

The minutes and a video of each press conference are available at the following website:

https://www.federalreserve.gov/monetarypolicy/fomccalendars.htm

B) **Summary of Economic Projections**

Beginning in late 2007, Federal Reserve policymakers began publishing economic projections, known as the "Summary of Economic Projections," four times a year. Those projections, published along with the FOMC post-meeting statement, now provide participants' assessments of the most likely outcomes for real gross domestic product growth, the unemployment rate, inflation, and the federal funds rate over the medium term and over the longer run. Here is a guide to what is in the SEP:

https://www.federalreserve.gov/monetarypolicy/guide-to-the-summary-of-economic-projections.htm

C) **Testimonies to Congress**

By statute, the Federal Reserve Chair testifies twice each year on economic developments and monetary policy before the congressional committees that oversee the Federal Reserve. At those times, the Board of Governors presents the semiannual Monetary Policy Report to Congress, which discusses the conduct of monetary policy, economic developments, and prospects for the future.

1.5 The Fed's Three Primary Tools for Policy Implementation

1.5.1 The Fed Funds Rate

"Changes in short-term market interest rates resulting from a change in the FOMC's target for the federal funds rate typically are transmitted to medium- and longer-term interest rates, such as those

on Treasury notes and bonds, corporate bonds, fixed-rate mortgages, and auto and other consumer loans. Medium- and longer-term interest rates are also affected by how people expect the federal funds rate to change in the future. For example, if borrowers and lenders think, today, that the FOMC is likely to raise its target for the federal funds rate substantially over the next several years, then medium-term interest rates today will be appreciably higher than short-term interest rates."

- from <u>The Federal Reserve System Purposes & Functions</u>

Notice from the following chart how the Fed dropped the Fed Funds rate during prominent times of weakness in the economy:

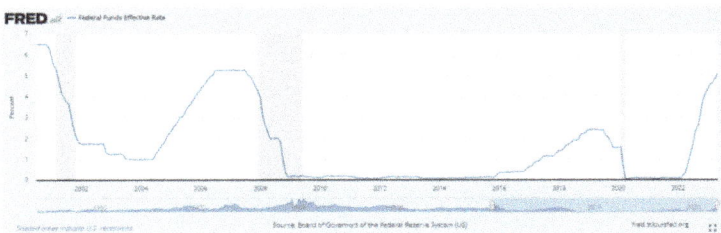

The grey vertical bars show recessions. The Fed has taken decisive action to lower the fed funds rate to near zero in each case.[6] In the paragraph below on Quantitative Easing, you will see that the drop in the Fed Funds rate was part of a larger strategy that also included Quantitative Easing.

1.5.2. Quantitative Easing and Tightening

Quantitative Easing (QE) is a form of monetary policy in which a central bank, like the U.S. Federal Reserve, purchases securities from the open market to reduce interest rates and increase the money supply. Quantitative easing creates new

---

[6] Source: https://fred.stlouisfed.org/series/fedfunds

bank reserves, providing banks with more liquidity and encouraging lending and investment.

Quantitative easing is often implemented when short-term interest rates are near zero and economic growth is stalled. Without the ability to lower rates further, central banks can strategically increase the money supply. To execute quantitative easing, the Fed buys government bonds and other securities from financial institutions and/or the open market, thereby injecting bank reserves into the economy. This results in an increase in the money supply, a lowering of interest rates for longer-term bonds, and provides liquidity to the banking system, allowing banks to lend at lower rates.

Note: Chapter 2, Bond Basics, will describe the relationship between bond purchases and the resulting changes to the long-term interest rates.

Quantitative Easing has been implemented four times, which are named QE1, QE2, QE3, and QE4.

QE1 started in November 2008

QE2 started in November 2010

QE3 started in September 2012

QE4 started in March 2020

The first use in 2008 was in response to the housing crisis of 2007 and 2008. Before the crisis, interest rates were very low, and banks promoted home purchases by packaging and selling home loans to generate more funds to lend as mortgages. Mortgages were offered to applicants with questionable incomes and payment histories. Many subprime mortgage holders defaulted on their loans. Some banks faced the risk of default, and home prices plummeted.

The logic behind creating Quantitative Easing is eloquently described in a speech by Ben Bernanke, then Chairman of the Board of the Federal Reserve System, in 2012. Interested readers can find this historical speech at the following link:

www.federalreserve.gov/newsevents/speech/bernanke20121120a.pdf

Quantitative tightening (QT) is a contractionary monetary policy tool used by central banks to reduce the liquidity or money supply in the economy. A central bank carries out quantitative tightening by selling the financial assets it holds on its balance sheet into the financial markets, which lowers asset prices and increases interest rates. QT is the opposite of quantitative easing (QE). The main goal of QT is to normalize, or raise, interest rates to prevent rising inflation by making borrowing more expensive and reducing demand for goods and services in the economy.[7]

The most recent implementation of QT started in January of 2022. By that time, inflation had risen very dramatically and was far above the Fed's 2% target. To rein in inflation, the Fed began selling bonds from its portfolio, thereby depressing long-term bond prices. This resulted in a dramatic increase in long-term interest rates, a goal of QT.

We will see in Section II of this book how QE and QT are highly exploitable from an investment perspective. To put it more forcefully, a strategic investor must be aware of QE and QT, because these major events will significantly impact bond prices and stocks as well.

1.5.3 The Money Supply

The money supply is generally defined as a collection of safe assets that households and businesses can use for payments or as

---

[7] Source: Wikipedia

short-term investments. For instance, U.S. currency and balances in checking and savings accounts are included in many measures of the money supply. Several standard measures exist, such as the monetary base, M1, and M2. M2 is frequently used, and its components include cash on hand, money in checking accounts, savings accounts, and other short-term savings options like certificates of deposit (CDs).

Quantitative Easing is one cause of increases in the money supply. As the Fed purchases long-term bonds (QE), the cash from the Fed flows into the banking system. Notice in the graph below how much M2 increased in 2020 as the Fed started QE4 and dropped the Fed Funds rate to near zero:

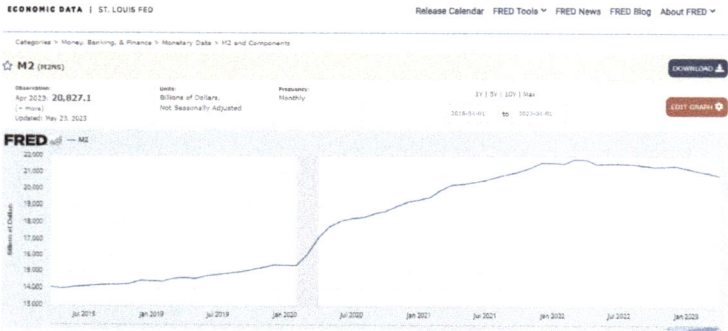

At certain periods, measures of the money supply have exhibited fairly close relationships with key economic variables, such as nominal gross domestic product (GDP) and the price level. Based partly on these relationships, some economists— Milton Friedman being the most famous example—have argued that the money supply provides important information about the near-term course for the economy and determines the level of prices and inflation in the long run. Central banks, including the

Federal Reserve, have at times used measures of the money supply as an important guide in the conduct of monetary policy.[8]

Now that we have discussed Quantitative Easing and the Money Supply, let's look at the effects that QE4 had on the economy. QE4 was initiated in March 2020, when it became clear that COVID-19 was a pandemic and would have a major negative impact on the economy. The Fed bought large numbers of U.S. treasuries, and this provided a major cash influx into the economy. Below, we will see two graphs. The first shows how the Fed's ownership of bonds increased dramatically starting in March 2020:

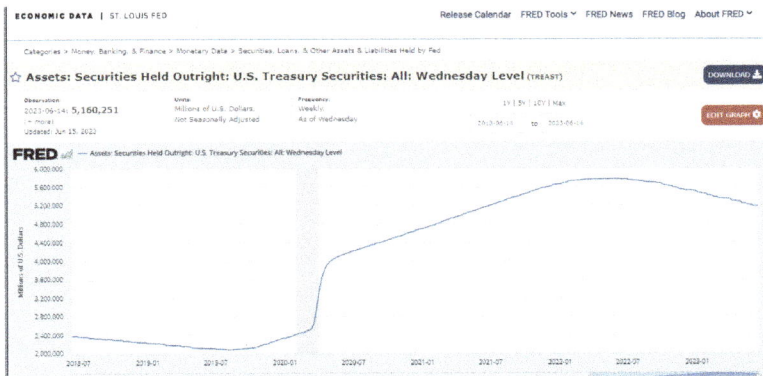

The next graph shows how the money supply, measured by M2, grew as a result:

[8] Source: https://www.federalreserve.gov/faqs/money_12845.htm

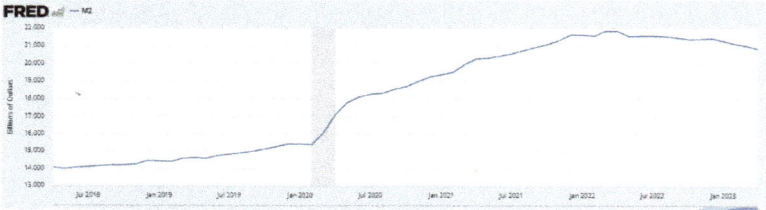

Lastly, let's look at how pumping cash into the economy led to excessive inflation.

When the money supply is greatly increased, as it was starting in 2020, banks increased funds to lend to businesses and individuals. The availablily of funds at low rates of interests promotes purchases of autos, homes, and investment by businesses. Inflation was the result, exacerbated by lower tax rates on individuals and businesses

As you can see, the inflation we had starting in 2020 was not a surprise to anyone watching the growth of the money supply.

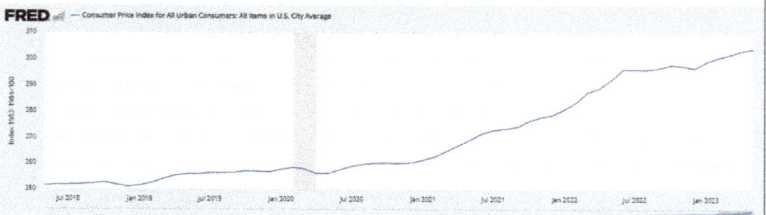

You will find more information in Section II on how strategic investors can utilize Fed announcements and actions to inform their investment decisions. An example of how following the Fed can be profitable is as follows:

14

1.6 An Example Opportunity for Fed Watchers

Minutes of the FOMC meetings and videos of the chairman's press conferences are available   at this link:

https://www.federalreserve.gov/monetarypolicy/fomccalendars.htm

Starting in January 2022 and for the remainder of 2022, the meetings communicated that interest rates would rise to control inflation and continue to rise until substantial evidence showed that inflation was moderating significantly. Hence, the strategic investor knew that bond prices would fall in response to the rising interest rates. (See Chapter 2 on Bonds).

In March 2022, the Fed Funds Rate was 0.2%. During the March 16 presentation by Fed Chairman Powell, he presented the following chart showing future projections of the fed funds rate. As you can see, it projected the fed funds rate to be close to 3% by the end of 2022.[9]

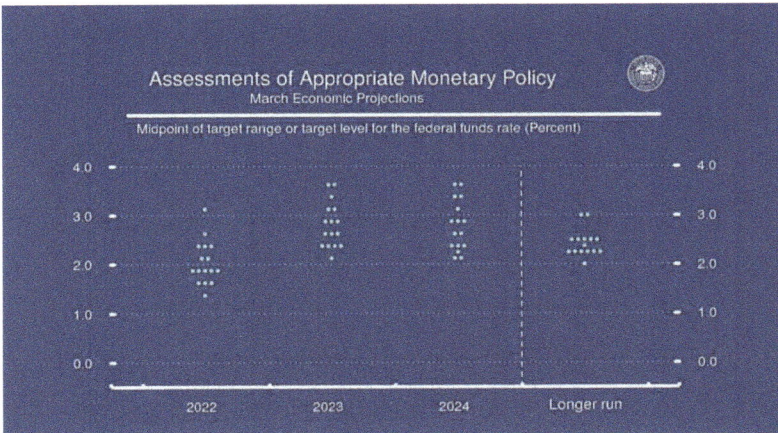

[9] Source:
https://www.federalreserve.gov/monetarypolicy/fomcpresconf20220316.htm

This represents a huge increase in the fed funds rate, and the projections were realized. See the following chart showing increases that actually occurred:

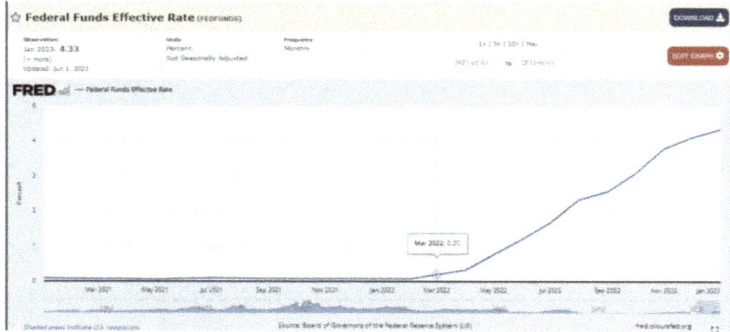

The Fed clearly stated that interest rates would be increasing significantly in an effort to curb and reverse the rising inflation. The strategic investor took note of that and was very cautious about long stock positions, but he also realized that bond prices would drop as a result of the interest rate increases. (See Chapter 2 Bond Basics). He might well have bought TBF, an exchange-traded fund that rises when bond prices fall. Take a look at its chart below from Barchart.com:

The Fed virtually told the perceptive listener what the result would be!

During 2022, the fund price went from $16.50 to $21.50, an increase of 30%.

During the same time, the S&P 500 index dropped 20%!

Chapter 2: Bond Basics

You may wonder why this chapter on Bond Basics precedes the two following chapters on equities. The reasons are:

1) The actions of the Fed as described in Chapter 1, can have both immediate and long-lasting effects on bond prices, and a basic understanding of bonds is necessary to capitalize on these changes.

2) The future movement of bond prices is often easier to predict than that of equity prices, especially given the Fed's policy of describing changes to the Fed Funds Rate far in advance.

3) The availability of bond-based ETFs makes investing in bonds much easier than before.

4) Section II on Strategy covers investing in bonds, and understanding the basics is essential for these strategies.

2.1 Types of Bonds

1) <u>U.S. government fixed-income securities.</u>

The three most common types of treasuries are Treasury Bills (T-Bills), Treasury Notes (T-Notes) and Treasury Bonds (T-Bonds). Treasury Bills are short-term investments that mature in less than one year. Treasury Notes have maturities of 2,3,5,7 or 10 years and are considered intermediate in duration. Treasury Bonds are issued with maturities of 20 and 30 years and are considered long-duration bonds. U.S. Treasury notes and bonds pay interest every six months. Treasury Bills do not pay interest; the selling price at maturity includes the agreed-upon interest. In addition to the most common

18

types mentioned above, there are also Savings Bonds and Treasury Inflation Protected Securities (TIPS). We will focus on the big 3: T-Bills, T-Notes, and T-Bonds.

Buying Treasuries:

You can buy treasuries directly from the government at:

https://www.treasurydirect.gov/marketable-securities/treasury-notes/.

There is a great deal of information on this website about rates, types of treasuries and how to purchase. You can also buy treasuries from a bank or broker.

2) <u>Inflation-Adjusted Treasury Bonds.</u> These bonds are commonly called TIPS, which stands for Treasury Inflation-Protected Securities. They are unique because the face value adjusts for changes in the Consumer Price Index. For example, if you bought a TIPS with a face value of $10,000 and the CPI increases by 3% during the next year, your bond's face value now becomes $10,300. If the coupon rate is 2%, the coupon payments are now calculated on the new face value, and hence increase by 3% in dollar amount from what they initially were. The 2% coupon rate remains the same, but it's based on a larger face value. There are two coupon payments per year, on six-month intervals. TIPS are available in three maturities: 5, 10, and 30 years.

3) <u>Corporate fixed income securities.</u>

These are issued by corporations to provide capital for their operations and/or expansion. They are also issued to finance debt. Corporate bonds generally pay higher interest than treasuries, as treasuries are considered to have zero risk of default.

The difference between the rates of highly rated corporates and treasuries is called the "credit spread." Corporate bonds are rated by one or more of the three U.S. rating agencies: Standard & Poor's Global Ratings, Moody's Investor Services and Fitch Ratings. The highest rating is triple A, and the lowest is "junk."

4) Bonds without coupons-Zeros

Zeros are bonds that do not pay periodic interest payments (coupons). These bonds are sometimes issued by corporations. The U.S. government does not issue zeros. However, some bond dealers buy U.S. treasuries, remove the coupons, and resell the bonds without coupons. (They keep the coupons and collect the interest payments, or package them and sell them to investors). These are Zeros, and also called STRIPS, which stands for Separate Trading of Registered Interest and Principal of Securities. Zeros sell at a deep discount to bonds with coupons. That is so because the buyer of zeros benefits only from the difference between the market price of the bond and its face value (Face Value is the amount the bond pays the owner at maturity). The lower price than compensates for the lack of interest payments. We will explore some differences between the coupon bonds and zeros in the following paragraphs on Duration and Yield to Maturity.

5) Tax Free Bonds

These are bonds issued by states or municipalities that are not subject to federal income tax. They are commonly called "Munis" short for municipal bonds. They are of interest primarily to high-income investors. You will pay state tax in some states, but not in all. Some states exempt bonds from their own state, but do tax income from bonds issues outside of their state. Tax-free bonds pay noticeably less interest than other bonds. To calculate whether tax-free bonds will be advantages for you, consider the following formula from Investopedia.com

Tax Equivalent Yield = Tax-Free Yield / (1 – Tax Rate).

Translation: That's the yield that the muni must have in addition to its federal tax-free status to be equal to the yield of a corporate bond. As you can see, if your tax rate is high, the muni will compare favorably with another bond with the Tax Equivalent Yield (tax rate above should include federal and state tax if your state will tax the income, otherwise not).[10]

2.2 Duration

There are two types of Duration.

The first is Macaulay duration, which is the weighted average time until all the bond's cash flows are paid. Bond calculators online will often compute this automatically. When you buy a newly issued 10-year bond with no coupons (a Zero), its duration is 10 years. After holding it for 2 years, its duration decreases to 8 years. For bonds with coupons, Macaulay duration is less than that of Zeros because interest payments are made earlier than the principal at maturity. These interest payments lower the weighted average of cash flows since they happen periodically, whereas Zeros only have a payment at maturity.

---

[10] source of the above paragraph:
https://www.investopedia.com/articles/investing-strategy/090116/think-twice-buying-taxfree-municipal-bonds.asp

The second type of duration is called Modified Duration. Modified duration is not measured in years; instead, it measures the expected percentage change in a bond's price to a 1% change in interest rates. As we will see, bonds with longer time to maturity are much more susceptible to interest changes than those with shorter time to maturity. For details on the formulas, see Investopedia.com and search on Duration.

Calculating Duration:

We will use the calculator at the link below to see how long bonds are much more sensitive to interest rate changes than short bonds.

https://www.mymathtables.com/calculator/finance/bond-duration-calculator.html

First, we will look at a coupon bond with a 5-year maturity.

Yield To Maturity   Market Price

Bond Face Value/Par Value ($)
1000

Years to Maturity
5

Annual Coupon Rate (%)
1.5

Yield to Maturity (Market Yield) (%)
6.5

Coupon Payment Frequency
○ Monthly   ● Twice a Year
○ Quarterly   ○ None (Zero Coupon)
○ Annually

Calculate   Clear

Results

Current Market Price ($) = 789.44
Macaulay Bond Duration = 4.8 Years
Modified Bond Duration (Δ%/1%) = 4.66

When we hit "Calculate, the results appear. According to the above, if interest rates increase by 1% (from 6.5% to 7.5%), the bond price will drop by 4.66%

Now, let's look at a similar bond with 20 years to maturity:

Yield To Maturity   Market Price

Bond Face Value/Par Value ($)
1000

Years to Maturity
20

Annual Coupon Rate (%)
1 5

Yield to Maturity (Market Yield) (%)
6 5

Coupon Payment Frequency

○ Monthly
○ Quarterly
○ Annually

● Twice a Year
○ None (Zero Coupon)

Calculate   Clear

Results

Current Market Price ($) = 444.79
Macaulay Bond Duration = 15.6 Years
Modified Bond Duration (Δ%/1%) = 15.08

Now, if interest rates increase by 1% (from 6.5% to 7.5%), the bond price will drop by 15.08%! Yikes! In 2022, interest rates rose dramatically, and long bonds dropped greatly. Banks typically hold large amounts of U.S. treasuries, often long-duration bonds. This significantly impacted the bank's balance sheets in 2022.

2.3 Yield to Maturity (YTM)

This metric for bonds helps us understand the pricing of bonds, so we will discuss it now and why it matters. Yield to Maturity is an estimate of the total rate of return expected by an investor who purchases a bond at a specific market price and holds it until maturity. During that period, the investor receives and reinvests all interest payments and then receives the face value of the bond at maturity. In the previous section on Duration, the calculator used Yield to Maturity in the duration calculations. Looking again at the 20-year bond above, the yield to maturity is 6.5% for the bond with 20 years remaining.

So, this bond, if held to maturity, yields a return similar to a CD, assuming one could be found paying 6.5% per year. Yes, you are correct that CDs are not offered that last for 20 years.

2.4 Pricing of Bonds and Bond Portfolios

Next, let's use the calculator to find the fair market price of a bond with known (published) yield to maturity and coupon rates. If a bank or broker is offering a bond you're interested in, but you want to verify that the price they are asking is fair. For example, the 20-year bond in section 2.2 can be reconsidered. When we click on Calculate, the results show that the Current Market Price was $444.79. Don't pay much more than this for the bond!

2.5 Bond ETFs and Portfolios of Bonds

Investing in bonds has become easier now that Exchange Traded Funds (ETFs) are widely accessible. Purchasing individual bonds can be tedious due to the many different maturities and yields available. Let's examine three bond ETFs. First, TLT, a fund managed by BlackRock iShares. This ETF, the iShares 20+ Year Treasury Bond ETF, aims to track the investment results of an index made up of U.S. Treasury bonds with remaining maturities longer than twenty years. Here is a two-year chart of TLT;

Symbol | Period
TLT | Weekly ▾ | Update | 🔍 Inspect ☐

TLT iShares 20+ Year Treasury Bond ETF Nasdaq GM + BATS   ® StockCharts.com
9-May-2023 11:23am   Open 103.61 High 103.87 Low 103.32 Last 103.47 Volume 25.5M Chg -1.42 (-1.35%) ▾
W TLT (Weekly) 103.47

There is a lot to learn from this chart. (Generated on StockCharts.com as a weekly chart)

First, how did people fare in 2022 who believed in the long-held theory that, in a down market for stocks, bonds are much safer? When the stock market began its slide in January 2022, the TLT ETF was at $140 per share. At the close of 2022, it was at $102. This represents a loss of $38.00 per share and a 27% decline. Painful, I know. Especially because the FED told us that interest rates would be raised significantly in 2022 to combat inflation, they even predicted the timing and magnitude of the rate increases. You can see why this chapter comes before the one on the Federal Reserve System.

If you had already understood the concepts in this chapter and the one on the Fed, you might have invested in anticipation of rising rates. This can be achieved by shorting the TLT, but it is not necessary. There is another ETF, TBF. It is managed by ProShares. The ProShares Short 20 Plus Year Treasury seeks daily investment results, before fees and expenses, that correspond to the inverse (-1x) of the daily performance of the ICE U.S. Treasury 20 Plus Year Bond Index. ICE is short for the Intercontinental Exchange. (see theice.com, a provider of many market indices) So, rather than short TLT, you could have bought the TBF ETF at the beginning of 2022 when the Fed announced its intention to raise interest rates during most of 2022.

Here is a 2-year chart of TBF from StockCharts.com:

As an inverse ETF, it rises when bonds prices fall. If you bought it at the start of 2022 at $16.50 per share, by the end of 2022, it was trading at 21.50 for a profit of 31%.

In Section II on strategies, we will discuss Age-Related Funds.

As we discussed earlier, bonds with short durations fluctuate less in price than bonds with longer durations. So, during 2022, a long-duration inverse fund like TBF was just right; a as short-duration fund, like SHY, would not be effective.

This is a 2-year chart of SHY. Note how the variation in prices is much less than that of TLT or TBF. During 2022, SHY dropped from 83.50 to 80.75. This was a drop of 3.3%

Here is a two-year chart of SHY:

2.6 The U.S. Treasury Yield Curve

This yield curve is a graph that shows the interest rates of U.S. Treasuries, ranging from 1 month to 30 years in maturity, as of a particular date. It tells a lot about the economy at the time it is created, including investor expectations for the future of the economy and interest rates. It can be seen for the present or any date in the past on this website:

https://www.ustreasuryyieldcurve.com/.

The app at this link uses data from the government website https://home.treasury.gov/ and from https://fred.stlouisfed.org/

As of this writing, the yield curve is the following:

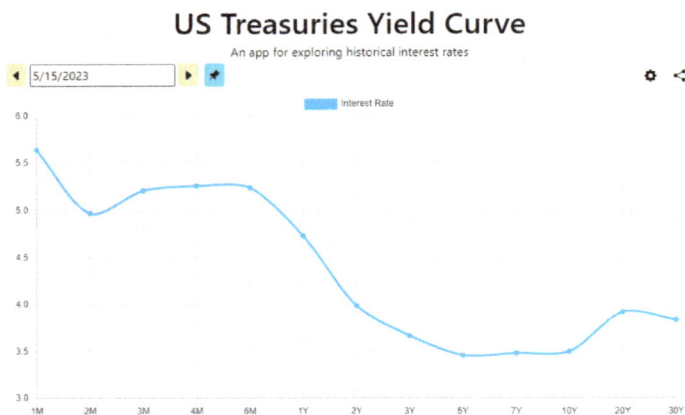

US Treasuries Yield Curve
An app for exploring historical interest rates

This is an atypical yield curve. It is not common for the graph to slope downwards, indicating longer-term rates are lower than short-term rates. This is known as an inverted yield curve and is often a precursor to an economic slowdown, or even a recession.

An example of a normal yield curve is the following from 5/12/2017

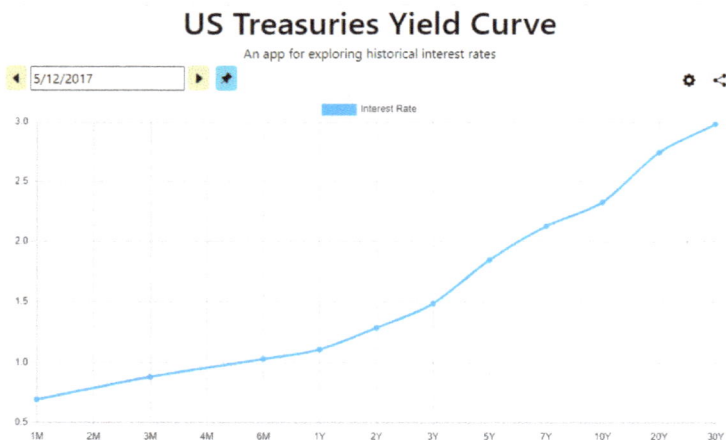

US Treasuries Yield Curve
An app for exploring historical interest rates

This upsloping graph is called a normal yield curve because throughout history, long-term rates have typically been higher than short-term rates. The logic here is that since short-term bonds have almost no risk (they will mature soon), they pay less interest than long-term bonds, which may fluctuate very considerably, as we saw was the case in 2022. Investors in long-term bonds want and need to be compensated for that risk. Another reason for the upsloping graph is that in an expanding economy, interest rates often rise, and long-term rates anticipate this phenomenon. Investors will not buy a long-term bond that pays rates as low as those of short-term instruments when the odds are that rates will rise, and hence long-term bonds will likely fall in value. This is partly why we discussed duration at length.

Economists look not only at the yield curve, but also at the spread between the 10-year bond rates and the 2-year or 3-year rates. The 10-year is often used when examining interest rate spreads because mortgage rates correlate most closely to the 10-year rate. The 10-year /2-year spread offers a clear view of the yield curve's slope. The St Louis Fed website at this link shows the 10yr/2yr spread: https://fred.stlouisfed.org/series/T10Y2Y#

This very interesting graph is shown here:

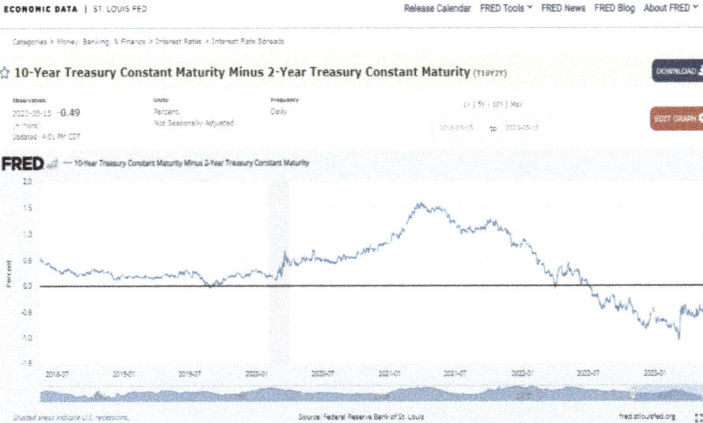

Note the inversion that started on March 30, 2022. Investors take inversion as yellow flags and that is reasonable based upon analysis of past inversions.

Note that the inversion started in July 2022, and as of this writing in May 2023, it remains inverted. Many economists view an inverted yield curve as a sign of an upcoming recession. The data supports this, as no recent recession was not preceded by a yield curve inversion. However, certain factors disturb the yield curve and reduce its reliability in predicting the economy's current and future state. In Chapter I, we saw how the Fed lowered the Fed Funds Rate to zero during periods of high recession risk. When the Fed does this, it forces the 2-year rate to be artificially low, which can increase the 10-year/2-year spread. During quantitative easing, the Fed buys long-term treasuries (see Chapter I), causing long bonds to rise in price and yields to fall. Therefore, both quantitative easing and tightening unnaturally disturb the yield curve by affecting the long end.

As of January 2024, the New York Fed provides the following graph. It displays the 10-year/3-year interest rate spread and includes grey vertical bars indicating recessions.[11]

[11] Source:
https://www.newyorkfed.org/medialibrary/media/research/capital_markets/Prob_Rec.pdf

Treasury Spread: 10 yr bond rate-3 month bill rate
Monthly Average (Percent)

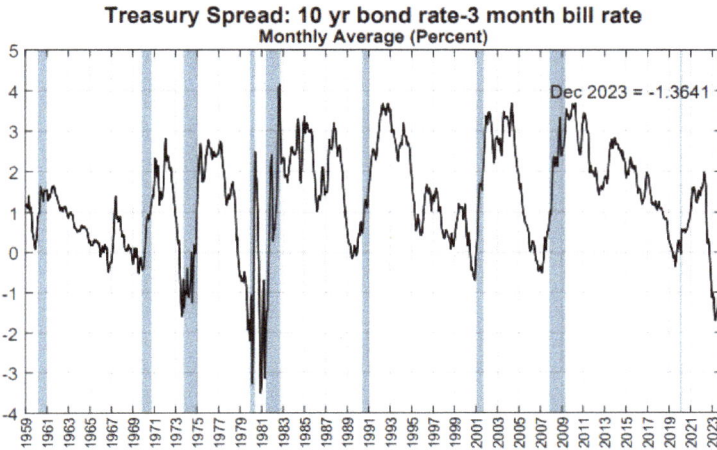

Dec 2023 = -1.3641

You will notice that the oft-heard assertion that recessions are always preceded by yield curve inversions, is largely corroborated by this data. Each vertical bar is preceded by the spread falling below zero. However, you will also notice that the converse of the assertion is not always true; i.e., not all occurrences of the treasury spread falling below zero are followed by a recession.

The yield curve inverted in November 2022 and has remained so since (as of January 2024). Some investment funds missed the rally of the Fall of 2023 because they were sure that a recession was imminent.

You will hear lots of commentary on the yield curve in the financial press, and hopefully, after reading this chapter, that discussion is clearer. Some of that discussion may overlook certain points we have made here, and you should also be prepared for that. There is a wealth of data and analysis of the yield curve available for your study if you choose to explore this topic further.

Chapter 3: Charts and Technical Analysis

First, where does this fit in the broader context? We will see in Sections II and III that when we are considering investments in stocks or bonds, we will use three views of the landscape. The broadest view, the macroeconomic view, which the Fed helps us understand, is first. Next, when selecting stocks that are good candidates, we will look at "fundamental analyses", which help us assess the value and prospects of good companies. Having selected solid candidates, we will use "Technical Analysis" to filter out stocks that are great candidates, but for which the time is not right. We will identify entry and exit points using Technical Analysis. Fortunately, there are great tools available on the web that help us with both technical and fundamental analyses. This holistic approach is aligned with what we discussed in the Introduction regarding structured decision-making.

3.1 Chart Styles and Sources of Charts

The two most common chart styles are bar charts and candlestick charts. Point and figure charts were used somewhat in the past but are not commonly used today. Here is one example of each, bar charts and candlesticks. Both are for Apple Stock. We will be using bar charts in this text. They are also called OHLC charts, which stand for Open, High, Low, Close. The chart below is a daily chart, and each bar shows the price action on that day. The opening price is indicated by a short horizontal line extending from the left side of the bar. The closing price is shown as a short horizontal line on the right side of each bar. The top of each bar is the high for the day, and the bottom is the low.

As the user moves the cursor over the chart, the values for the selected bar appear in the box shown above. One can choose the time interval such that each bar is one day, one week, one month, or even shorter intervals, such as 5 minutes. We will use daily and weekly charts in this book. Day-traders use shorter intervals than one day, and as we said in the introduction, day trading is not within the scope of this book. There are many charting services and some of them are free. The charts shown here are from Barchart.com. Barchart is an excellent source for charts, offering easy-to-use features, a variety of chart views, and technical overview opinions based on its automated technical analysis. StockCharts.com is also an excellent source for charts. For most of our readers, Barchart.com is the best choice, so we will describe how to chart in Barchart and use its great features. Barchart has a couple of advantages over StockCharts:

1) The user interface is simpler and clearer.

2) With a free membership, you can save chart templates so that you do not have to customize each chart to your preferred views. Saving templates in StockCharts requires a paid subscription.

3.1.1 Using Barcharts.com

When you go the barcharts.com, this is the top of the screen that will appear:

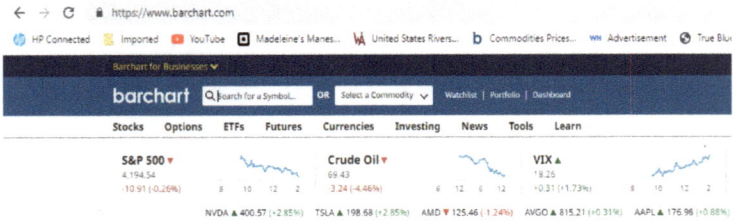

Enter the stock symbol in the window at the top left, "Search for a Symbol." For our example, we will enter AAPL, the ticker symbol for Apple, Inc. This is what appears when you hit Enter:

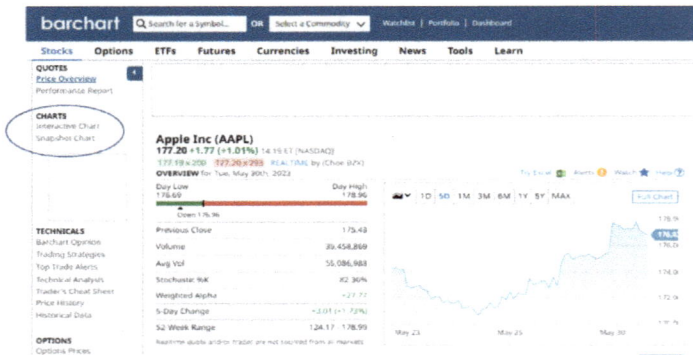

One can add technical indicators, or studies to any chart from either source. Both have a drop-down list below the chart for selecting the indicator(s) you wish to use. Barchart calls them Technical Studies, StockCharts calls them Indicators.

Market technicians use bar charts to assess the directional strength of the price, to identify buy points, and to identify points at which they would exit a long position should the price drop. (A long position is owning and equity in hopes of increasing prices.) We will discuss the use of charts more in the chapter on Equities.

I encourage readers to become familiar over time with some of technical studies available, but we will use Moving Averages as our primary tool either singly or two in combination.

This screen gives some basic information about the stock and also lists a menu of choices on the left. Note the circled choices which allow you to display charts. We will use the snapshot chart, You are welcome to also check out the interactive chart. When we select Snapshot Chart, this is the result:

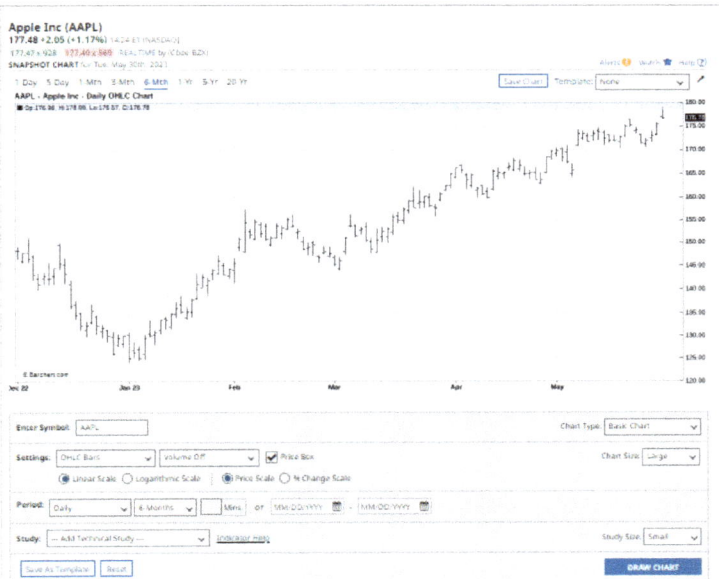

Below the chart is a menu of choices to tailor the chart to your preferences. Here is a closer look at that menu:

As you can see, this is a daily chart showing 6 months of data. We could have selected other time frames, including one year, a number of months, or year-to-date. Had we selected Weekly instead of Daily, the timeframe choices would be 1,2,3,4 or 5 years.

Please go to Barchart.com and create a chart; then modify the timeframe. Notice that using the MM/DD/YYY windows, you can even create a chart of just a period of interest. For example, you could create a chart that shows data from 1 October 2019 to 31 October 2019 if you wished.

We haven't yet talked about Technical Studies. You may have noticed the box that allows you to select one or more Technical Studies. We will speak to this very shortly in Section 3.2 Technical Analysis.

Below is a Candlestick chart of AAPL. We will use bar charts, so this is here just for reference:

3.2 Technical Analysis

Technical analysis is the study of price, and sometimes volume, to identify trends in the price of a stock or the overall market trend. Charts are primary tools of the technical analyst, which is why we began this chapter discussing charts. The technical analyst adds indicators, also known as studies or overlays, to the chart to assist in identifying trends and finding low-risk entry points for buying stocks or ETFs (An ETF is an Exchange Traded Fund. For

Example, SPY is an ETF that tracks the S&P 500 index). There are analysts whose primary focus is technical analysis. One can even become a Chartered Market Technician, a designation provided by the CMT association after successfully passing a series of tests.

This book recommends Fundamental Analysis, discussed later, to determine economic trends, earnings prospects for individual companies, and to assess the current valuation of potential investments. In Section II of this book (Strategies), we recommend Technical Analysis to identify market trends, select entry and exit points, and in general, to give us the tools to add timing to the process of successful investing. As we will see in Sections II and III, there are many technical analysis tools available on the web to perform detailed assessments of the short, medium and long-term prospects for individual investments or for the markets in general. In this section, we will examine a few of the most commonly used technical analysis tools, primarily those that we will utilize in the strategy sections later. There are excellent books on Technical Analysis, and sources on the web, but our focus will not require an in-depth study of these sources, even though they are worthy as part of a long-term education about the markets and tools.

3.2.1 Moving Averages:

Moving Averages are primary in chart analysis. Let's look at a chart with a 20-day Moving Average superimposed on the chart.

The line represents the 20-bar moving average. It is calculated by summing the closing prices of the most recent 20 bars and dividing the total by 20. StockCharts.com and Barchart.com do this for you. The above chart, created in BarChart, was generated using the following menu after selecting SnapChart from the opening menu on the left. After clicking on "Add Technical Study," we selected "Simple Moving Average" from the upper choices called "Add an Overlay/Indicator." The second graphic below shows you how to select "Moving Average," Simple after clicking on "Add Technical Study."

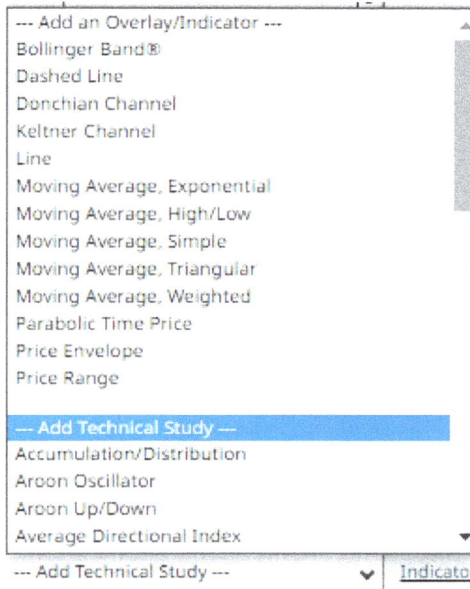

When you select "Simple Moving Average," 20 bars is the default. You can change the 20-bar calculation to any number you wish by clicking on the box just below the one labeled "Study." It now displays "Simple Moving Average" (20). When you click on it, the following appears:

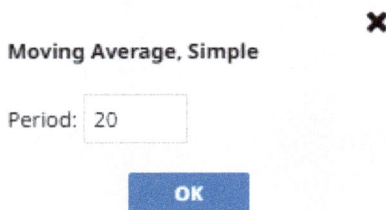

To create a 12-bar MA, just change the 20 to 12 and click OK. Then select Draw Chart to see the updated chart. The Draw Chart button is located below the chart on the bottom right. Shorter MAs (with less bars) highlight short-term trends, longer Mas highlight longer trends. We will discuss the strategic use of MAs in Sections II and III. Meanwhile, if you are not familiar with creating charts with MAs, please do so in BarChart.com.

In addition to Simple Moving Averages, you will see that there are also Exponential Moving Averages. These differ from Simple Moving Averages in that they give more weight to the most recent bars. For more details on EMAs, go to Investopedia.com and put EMA into the search box. We will use Simple Moving Averages in this text, but you are welcome to explore the differences between them and Exponential MAs.

In BarCharts, when you use the dropdown list called Add Technical Study, you will see two categories to choose from: Overlay/Indicator and Technical Study. Moving Averages are in the first category. Overlays/Indicators in a BarChart have the same scale as the price of the stock, ETF, or fund. They can go as high or as low as the prices on the chart. They are displayed on the chart itself, not below it, as are the Technical Studies shown as a second category below the Overlay/Indicator list.

The second category in BarChart, is called Technical Studies, studies that have ranges and which, over time, tend to revert to the mean. Examples are the Relative Strength Index, and MACD, Moving Average Convergence and Divergence. Technical studies that revert to the mean are commonly called "Oscillators". This is the topic we address next, following the discussion of Moving Averages.

3.2.2 Oscillators:

Oscillators are technical studies that fluctuate in a range, as opposed to stock prices and overlays/indicators that may increase without bounds. Typically, oscillators are used by chartists to identify when a trend is in place and when it is losing momentum. They can also be used to identify when a stock is oversold or overbought. We will illustrate the use of two of the most commonly used oscillators, the Relative Strength Index (RSI) and Moving Average Convergence and Divergence (MACD).

Relative Strength Index (RSI):

The Relative Strength Index (RSI) is a momentum oscillator that measures the rate of change in the price of the stock or ETF being analyzed. The RSI oscillates between zero and 100. The RSI is indicating an oversold condition when it is below 30 and an overbought condition when it is above 70. When a stock is in an uptrend, the RSI will typically be between 40 and 80. During a downturn, the RSI typically ranges from 10 to 50.

Let's look at a chart of Tesla stock along with the RSI values as well. We will use a chart with a one-year duration. This is the one-year chart:

Two excellent books for further study:

Top 7 Books to Learn Technical Analysis for Stocks (investopedia.com)

Technicians who use the Relative Strength Index are looking for overbought and oversold conditions, as we mentioned, and they also look for other conditions. Divergence is one of these. In the graph above, the ellipse highlights a time when the RSI, shown above the price chart, is losing steam. It is experiencing lower highs, even as the price of TSLA is in a small range. This, to many technicians, indicates that the next move in the price of TSLA will be down. In this case, that certainly was true.

RSI can provide useful insights, but it must be used in conjunction with other analyses to result in trading signals. RSI can remain elevated for extended periods during bull markets, so high readings should indicate caution; however, a sell signal should require confirmation, such as a short-term moving average of the stock price turning down.

Moving Average Convergence/Divergence MACD:

This oscillator is calculated as the difference between two moving averages. The Moving Average Convergence/Divergence indicator is a momentum oscillator primarily used to identify trends. Unlike RSI, it is not used to identify overbought or oversold conditions. It appears on the chart as two lines. The first is the difference between two moving averages. In the chart below, we show the MACD (12, 26, 9). This means that two moving averages were used, a 12-bar MA and a 26-bar MA. The difference between the two MAs is one of the lines shown and is called the MACD line. The second line, called the Signal Line, is the 9-Bar MA of the first line. The crossover of these two lines provides trading signals. See the example below.[12]

Fidelity has published a wonderful set of descriptions of technical indicators. You may wish to look at this great resource. The top-level URL is Fidelity Learning Center: Technical Analysis Indicator Guide

---

[12] It is from this link:
https://www.fidelity.com/learning-center/trading-investing/technical-analysis/technical-indicator-guide/macd.

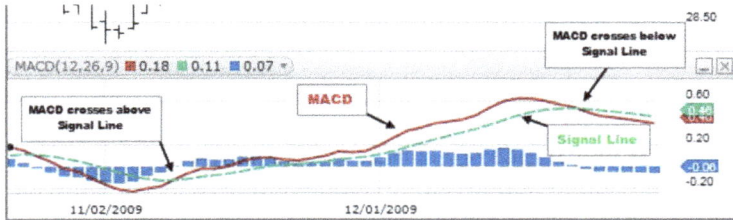

MACD(12,26,9) ■ 0.18 ■ 0.11 ■ 0.07 ▼

MACD crosses below
Signal Line

MACD

MACD crosses above
Signal Line

Signal Line

28.50

0.60

0.20

-0.20

11/02/2009   12/01/2009

Note that the graph above lists the parameters: MACD (12,26,9). This means the two moving averages were used in the calculation of MACD, 12-Bar and 26-Bar. The signal line is the 9-bar MA of the difference between the 12-bar MA and the 26-bar MA.

When the MACD line crosses from below to above the signal line, the indicator is considered bullish. The lower the starting point of the MACD line, the stronger the signal.

When the MACD line crosses from above to below the signal line, the indicator is considered bearish. The higher the starting point for the MACD line, the stronger the signal.

You will see from the following chart how effective the MACD can be in generating trading signals. I added vertical lines to the chart that show when the MACD line crossed the Signal line. No oscillator is accurate all the time, but that said, notice how valuable the signals were on this chart:

43

S&P 500 Index ($SPX)

The MACD can also be used to indicate which direction the market is likely to take while it is rangebound, i.e., it remains at a level for a short time. Let's illustrate the MACD, which provides guidance on a possible breakout. We will look at a one-year chart of Tesla:

The MACD line is black, and the signal line is red.

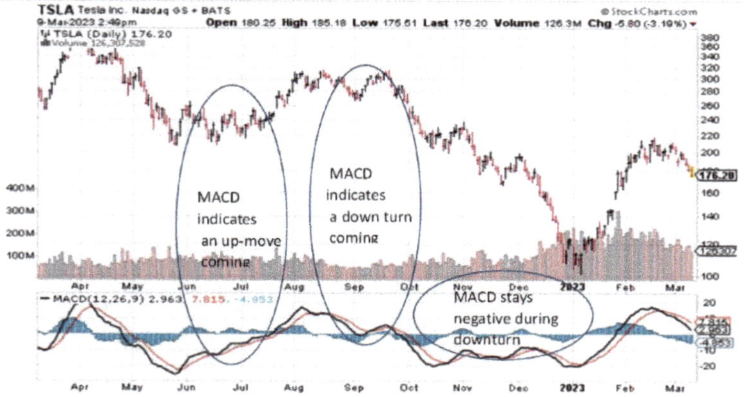

Support/Resistance

Mas

Trends (Trendlines and Mas)

Momentum Indicators   Oscillators (MACD, and RSI)

What Barchcart and StockCharts provide

I am asking you to understand the MACD at a high level primarily because some of the charting services use it in their assessments of the short-term, medium-term and long-term technical views of a stock or index. Barchart, in particular, uses it, so let's take a look at their applications of it.

Go to Barchart.com and enter AAPL in the "Search for a Symbol" box at the top. Then, select "Price Overview," the top entry from the list on the left side. This is what you will see:

We will focus on the "Barchart Technical Opinion" on the right. Notice the Strong Buy rating.

Now click on the Strong Buy banner, and this is what you will see next:

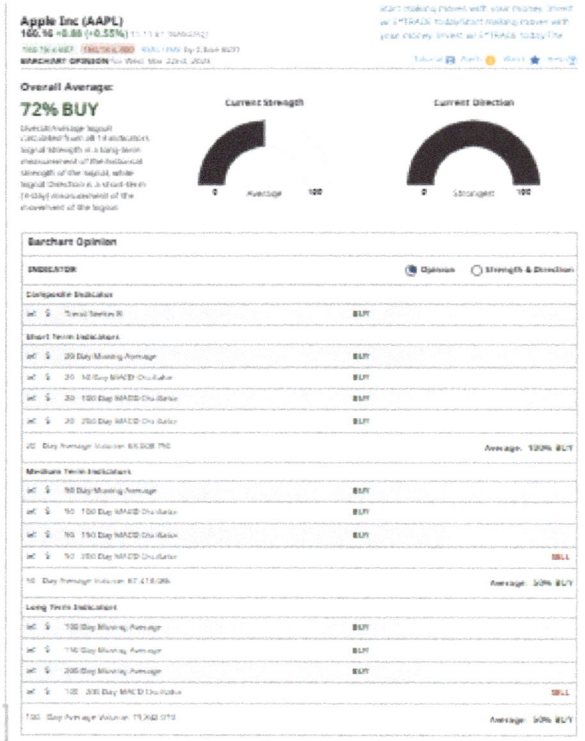

Note that there are ratings on short-term, medium-term and long-term. We will

discuss more on using this in the strategy section, but for now, you should notice

How moving averages and MACD are primary tools in their ratings on Barchart.

A question for you before our strategy discussions later in Section II: If you find a stock with strong earnings, promising future prospects, and it generally looks like a top choice for your portfolio, would you buy it now even if short-term indicators are saying "Sell" and a short-term Moving Average is pointing down?

Remember, timing is very important. Missing good entry points can turn what might be a short-term investment into a long-term recovery.

3.2.3 Trendlines, Support and Resistance

Charts will sometimes show that a certain price level has been reached multiple times on the upside without penetrating that level. When this occurs, that level is called Resistance, as the price has failed to advance through that level a number of times.

See this example from Investopedia:

Notice how $39 acts as resistance on Amazon.com's chart between March and November 2006.

Traders recognize that this level, just below $39.00 per share, has been a failure point on several occasions. Hence, many traders, if they wish to buy this stock, will wait until that resistance level has been breached. So many traders do this that there will be many buy orders at or close to $39.25 if that level is reached (using Buy on Stop orders). The result is a noticeable jump in price if that new high is reached. Because the price advance has failed previously just below $39.00, this level is considered a Resistance Level.

Interestingly enough, a similar phenomenon occurs when prices fail to penetrate a level multiple times on the downside. See this example also from Investopedia.[13]

Notice how the price has a difficult time falling below the support of $51.25.

Traders will place sell orders just below the level of $51.25 if they wish to exit or protect against further losses. These orders will also trigger a jump to the downside if the prior lows are breached. For this reason, and given the likelihood that a bounce will occur if the downside lows are not breached, this level is referred to as a Support Level.

The support and resistance levels mentioned above are examples of trendlines. Besides these, some market technicians also observe trendlines that are not horizontal. These can connect low points in an upward market or highs in a downward market.

See this example:

---

[13] https://www.investopedia.com/trading/support-and-resistance-basics/

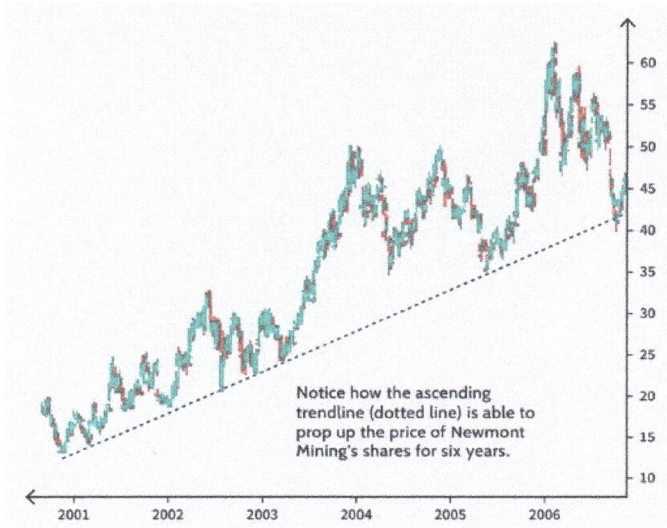

Notice how the ascending trendline (dotted line) is able to prop up the price of Newmont Mining's shares for six years.

Traders who own this stock may consider a penetration of the upsloping trendline, which could indicate a potential trend reversal. Although they are certainly followed, the horizontal Resistance and Support Trendlines are, in my opinion, more reliable and hence more important.

We will revisit this topic in the Strategy section, having described these technical tools here. As we mentioned earlier, we will utilize fundamental analysis, as described in Chapter 4, to select suitable candidates for investment. We will utilize Technical Analysis to determine our entry and exit points. Timing involves recognizing when entering or exiting would not be suitable.

If you would like to be aware of how effective Technical Analysis can be, look into the career of Larry Williams, author and legendary commodities trader. I trade commodities also, but I would never write a book on trading futures since Larry is the master and has published great books on the subject. Below is a paragraph from Wikipedia on Larry:

"Williams has created numerous market indicators, including Williams %R, Ultimate Oscillator, COT indices, accumulation/distribution indicators, cycle forecasts, market sentiment, and value measurements for commodity prices.[9][10] *Williams won the 1987 World Cup Championship of Futures Trading from the Robbins Trading Company, where he turned $10,000 to $1,137,600 (11,376%) in a 12-month competition with real money which is still the highest return ever in the World Cup."*

Chapter 4: Fundamental Analysis of Equities

This introductory paragraph is the same that we started with in Chapter 3:

First, where does this fit in the broader context? We will see in Sections II and III that when we are considering investments in stocks or bonds, we will use three views of the landscape. The broadest view, the macroeconomic view, which the Fed helps us understand, is first. Next, when selecting stocks that are good candidates, we will look at "fundamental analyses," which help us assess the value and prospects of good companies. Having selected solid candidates, we will use "Technical Analysis" to filter out stocks that are great candidates, but for which the time is not right. We will pick entry and exit points using Technical Analysis. Fortunately, there are great tools available on the web that help us with both technical and fundamental analyses. This holistic approach is part of what we mentioned in the Introduction regarding structured decision making.

4.1 Buying Part of a Company

This is the mindset of some of the most successful long-term investors, including Warren Buffett, Peter Lynch, Tom and David Gardner (Motley Fool). Short-term traders, including day traders do not have or need this view. This book is about investing, not trading, and we will embrace the same approach to stock selection as we would when considering buying the whole company (Something Warren Buffett has done on occasion). The fact that you are buying only 500 shares of a company with one million shares outstanding does not change the evaluation process. You still need to assess the company's near and long-term prospects, as well as whether the price is right.

4.1.1 Are You Qualified?

This is a question you may be asking yourself, and I would like to help you with your considerations. Here are some thoughts relevant to the question:

1) Approximately 80% of actively managed funds underperform the major indices. This figure has been published many times. Here is one reference:

   [New report finds almost 80% of active fund managers are falling behind (cnbc.com)](https://www.cnbc.com/2022/03/27/new-report-finds-almost-80percent-of-active-fund-managers-are-falling-behind.html)

   https://www.cnbc.com/2022/03/27/new-report-finds-almost-80percent-of-active-fund-managers-are-falling-behind.html

2) Fund managers are biased to hold stocks that are accepted by the community of analysts. There is a phrase in the investment industry, "You'll never lose your job losing your client's money on IBM." With that mindset, many funds will not invest in smaller growing companies that have great potential. The fact that funds are so late in investing in smaller companies is what Peter Lynch calls "Street Lag". You need not be disadvantaged by this phenomenon in your own stock selections.

3) There is a wealth of information available on any publicly traded stock. You can utilize this information to support your analysis.

4) After reading this book, you should have the necessary tools to gain confidence in yourself and your strategic approach to investing.

4.2 A Company Is An Earning Machine

If you have $10,000 to invest, you have alternatives including CDs, Bonds, and Equities. The macroeconomic view of the economy, as updated by the Fed, gives us great information on the best times to own stocks. We will discuss this further in Section II, Strategies, where we explore identifying the optimal times to hold long positions in stocks and those to limit your market exposure. In Section III, Putting It All Together, we will discuss how to perform asset allocation among cash, bonds, equities and real estate. For now, we are discussing how to evaluate equities in times that justify increasing our positions.

Some of the most important metrics in fundamental analysis relate to the earnings of the company. Here we will take a close look at 2 of the most important metrics and how to use them effectively. They are the P/E Ratio (Price-to-Earnings Ratio) and the PEG Ratio (Price-to-Earnings-to-Growth Ratio). As you will see, there are very important nuances to how these metrics are used.

4.2.1 Price to Earnings Ratio (P/E Ratio)

This is the most used metric, and one which lends itself to misuse by the uninitiated. This number is published on many websites for any listed stock. The definition of P/E is straightforward. Take the earnings of the company and divide them by the number of shares outstanding. This gives us earnings per share. Take the share price and divide it by this number to get the P/E ratio.

Let's look at the P/E ratio of Nvidia Corp. (NVDA) as shown on Barchart.com

Nvidia Corp (NVDA)
416.10 +5.93 (+1.45%) 09/22/23 [NASDAQ]
415.58 x 1 415.90 x 5 POST-MARKET **415.87 -0.23 (-0.06%)** 19:59 ET
QUOTE OVERVIEW for Fri, Sep 22nd, 2023   Try Excel Alerts Watch Help ?

Day Low	Day High
412.31	421.15

Open 415.72

			1D 5D 1M 3M 6M 1Y 5Y MAX	Full Chart
Previous Close	410.17			440.00
Volume	47,923,598			
Avg Vol	50,334,977			430.00
Stochastic %K	3.83%			420.00
Weighted Alpha	+193.10			416.10
5-Day Change	-22.90 (-5.22%)			410.00
52-Week Range	108.13 - 502.66		Sep 18 Sep 20 Sep 22	

Realtime quote and/or trades are not sourced from all markets.

Fundamentals   See More

Market Capitalization, $K	1,027,767,040	Price/Earnings ttm	93.86
Shares Outstanding, K	2,470,000	Earnings Per Share ttm	4.37
Annual Sales, $	26,974 M	Most Recent Earnings	2.70 on 08/23/23
Annual Income, $	4,368 M	Next Earnings Date	11/15/23

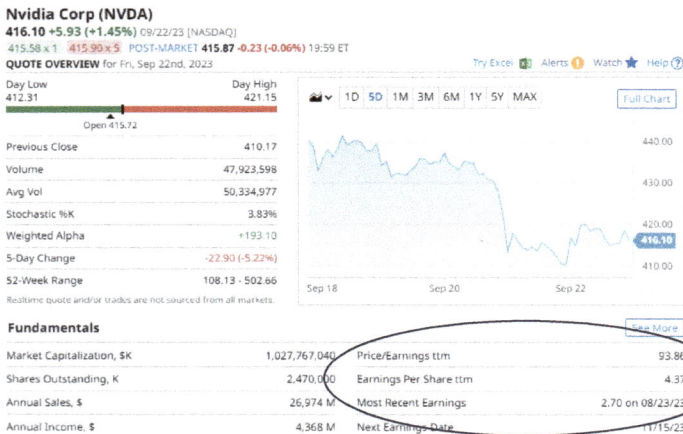

You will notice that the Price/Earnings is very high at 93.86. If the earnings stayed constant, it would take over 90 years for a share of stock to experience earnings equal to what that share cost. Clearly, the high P/E must be associate with the expectation of higher earnings. You will also notice that the letters "ttm" appear after Price/Earnings. Often overlooked, this term stands for "Trailing Twelve Months". For a stock like a utilities company, whose earnings do not change greatly year to year, this might be fine. For a company with strong earnings growth, it is not very useful. If you are considering NVDA as an investment, you might wish to consider what the P/E ratio is using a projection of future earnings.

Let's also look at Barchart's projection of future earnings. On the Barchart menu on the left, scroll down until you see ANALYSTS. Below that, select Earnings Estimates. This is what you will see:

Earnings Estimates

Next Earnings Release Date - 11/15/23	Current Qtr 10/2023	Next Qtr 01/2024	Fiscal Yr 01/2024	Fiscal Yr 01/2025
Average Earnings Estimate	2.99	3.29	9.46	14.43
Number of Estimates	13	12	14	13
High Estimate	3.06	3.46	9.77	17.62
Low Estimate	2.92	3.00	8.71	11.70
Prior Year	0.34	0.65	2.45	9.46
Growth Rate Est. (year over year)	+779.41%	+406.15%	+286.12%	+52.54%

Note that the yearly earnings ending January 2024 are $9.46 per share and for the year ending January 2025, are $14.43 per share. The above estimates are those shown in September 2023. Let's calculate what the P/E ratio would be in January 2025 if these estimates are realized. The P/E ratio if the stock price were still $416.10 would be $416.10/14.43 = 28.83. Certainly, the stock price might be substantially higher at that time, but the point here is that you, the investor, need to decide what earnings to use in calculating the P/E ratio. Last year's earnings may be stale, so you may wish to calculate the P/E ratio using the analysts' projections for next year or two years out, if available.

Note also that it can be meaningful to look at the P/E ratios of competitors. In Barchart, under "COMPANY" in the menu on the left, you can select "Competitors." You can look up their P/Es as well, or calculate them using earnings projections.

In addition to the P/E ratio being used for individual stocks, you will hear discussion of the P/E ratio of the market as a whole. The P/E ratio of the S&P 500 stocks is a frequent topic in the financial press. The easiest way to see it is by looking at the SPY ETF on Barchart. As of this writing, it is 17.86 ttm.

As we will see in the next graph, the P/E Ratio of the S&P500 correlates very strongly with the earnings of the S&P500 stocks. The graph shows both the P/E ratio and the 12-month recent earnings.

https://www.macrotrends.net/1324/s-p-500-earnings-history

This is a 20-year graph through Sept 2023. Red is earnings, blue is the S&P 500 index.

There are times when the P/E ratio gets way out of the norm, as seen in 2022. When Covid started, earnings estimates dropped significantly, as did actual earnings. Earnings dropped faster than stock prices, so the denominator in P/E shrank rapidly, elevating the ratio. This phenomenon was short-lived as stock prices continued to drop.

From the following chart, you will see that it is difficult to predict the course of the P/E ratio of the market. Considering the high correlation between earnings and the P/E, it is more useful to consider earnings estimates broadly in predicting changes to the P/E ratio.

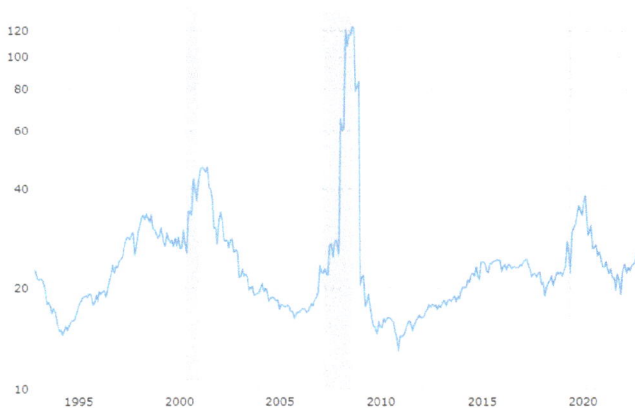

P/E of S&P 500 thru Sept 2023

One last thought on the P/E ratio of the broad market. If you invert it, you get E/P, which can be considered the yield of the stocks collectively in the S&P 500. It should, and almost always is, higher than the yield to maturity of the 10-Year U.S. Note. When bond yields rise, investment funds demand a higher yield from their stocks, or they would shift funds into bonds. The difference between stock yields and bond yields is often referred to as the "risk premium." There is no risk in holding U.S. government bonds. The risk premium is often close to 2%, which allows a person to calculate what the P/E ratio should be in a stable market without unusual economic circumstances. If the 10-year bond yield is 4%, and the risk premium is 2% that suggests the stock should yield 6%. That is equivalent to a P/E ratio of 100/6. or 16.67. As of this writing, the P/E of the S&P 500 is 17.86. The above paragraph is not to help you forecast the market, just to help you understand some constraints and guidelines.

4.2.2 PEG ratio – Price to Earnings to Growth:

In section 4.2.1, Price to Earnings Ratio, we mentioned how the P/E ratio of companies that are growing quickly, like NVDA, is very misleading when calculated on a trailing twelve-month basis. The fair stock price, in the minds of many analysts, is calculated using recent earnings and projected earnings. This methodology is fine, but earnings projections are somewhat subjective. Many analysts factor in a company's historical earnings growth when assessing the fair price of its stock. This has led to the development of a refined P/E ratio called the PEG ratio, which stands for Price to Earnings to Growth. It is worth your time to understand this useful metric.

First, how is the PEG ratio calculated? It's quite simple; you divide the P/E Ratio by the Growth Rate expected for the next five years. You can get an estimate of a stock's growth rate on finance.yahoo.com. Enter the stock symbol, and on the page that opens, select "Analysis". Scroll down and you will see "Growth Estimates". Below is what you would see for NVDA on October 2, 2023:

Growth Estimates	NVDA
Current Qtr.	443.10%
Next Qtr.	294.30%
Current Year	204.20%
Next Year	55.30%
Next 5 Years (per annum)	74.33%
Past 5 Years (per annum)	37.03%

The P/E ratio is 93.86 (very high), but the PEG ratio is 93.86/74.33 = 1.26. Many users of the PEG Ratio, including Motley Fool principals David and Tom Gardner, believe that the P/E Ratio of a growth stock should be approximately equal to its growth rate. This would correspond to a PEG ratio of 1.0.[14]

PEG ratios above 1 indicate that a stock is overpriced, and stocks with a PEG ratio below 1.0 are underpriced according to the traditional use of this metric. The PEG ratio is useful; we know that the P/E ratio should be higher for stocks that have higher earnings growth. But that is an unquantified axiom. The PEG ratio enables us to apply metrics to shed light on when a P/E ratio is too high or when the P/E ratio seems too low.

If you are not comfortable with a five-year projection of growth rate, use company projections, typically provided when earnings are announced, or information from other sources, even if they are for only 2 or 3 years. Projections as long as five years can be seen at finance.yahoo.com. Enter the stock symbol you wish, and select Analysis. Scroll down until you see the heading Growth Rates. There you will see the growth rate for the past 5 years and the projected growth rate for the next five years.

4.3 Time As A Factor in Picking Stocks

Four of the best-known value investors are Warren Buffett, Peter Lynch, David Gardner, and Tom Gardner. All four favor buying solid companies with the intention of holding them for years, not months. All four are interested in stocks with great prospects for growth over time and stocks that are fairly priced or underpriced. We have discussed how the P/E ratio and PEG ratio help us assess whether a stock is fairly priced. Given that earnings

---

[14] source: The Motley Fool Investment Guide Sept 2017 page 183

projections beyond five years are far less certain, I recommend not looking past 5 years when taking an initial position in a stock. It is difficult to predict how competition will change after five years; will the management team undergo significant changes? To be consistent with the lessons of the four value investors, look for stocks that you expect to hold for at least 3 years, and hopefully more. As time progresses, you may decide to keep a stock for much longer, or you may decide that your initial analysis needs to be revisited. You may decide to buy a stock of a company that is improving its competitive position.

4.3.1 Dealing With Major Bear Markets:

This is one topic where my experience and recommendations differ from those of the four value investors I mentioned above. In Section II of this book, Strategies for Equities, the discussion starts with the topic of Buy and Hold? (Chapter 5 section 5.1) The analysis in 5.1 shows that it is not necessary to endure the pain and suffering of most bear markets. It even presents a detailed methodology for determining when to exit the markets at the beginning of major downturns and when to re-enter. The coverage of the topic is probably new to most of you, including very seasoned investors.

Does the above paragraph (and section 5.1 mean that I don't share the philosophy of the value investors or their recommendations? Actually not; it presents a way to augment their techniques with risk avoidance during critical times, and it shows how these methods can improve your results in a very significant way.

The goal of most investment managers is to outperform the major indices. (most commonly the S&P 500 index.) It is probably your goal also, or you could just buy the S&P 500 ETF

"SPY" and be done with it. Avoiding all or part of bear markets is a way for you to outperform the indices.

For most of the time, when no bear market is in place (as defined in 5.1), I am completely aligned with the recommendations and methods of the value investors.

Berkshire Hathaway, the company whose CEO is Warren Buffett, went from a high of $361.00 per share on March 28, 2022, to a low of $260.00 on October 10, 2022. I love Berkshire Hathaway (ticker BRK.b), but I do not believe it was necessary to suffer this magnitude of loss in 2022.

4.4 The Size of a Company Matters

Let's recall a paragraph from section 4.1.1 earlier in this chapter:

Fund managers are biased to hold stocks that are accepted by the community of analysts. There is a phrase in the investment industry, "You'll never lose your job losing your client's money on IBM." With that mindset, many funds will not invest in growth-oriented companies having great potential. The fact that funds are so late in investing in smaller companies is what Peter Lynch calls "Street Lag". You need not be disadvantaged by this phenomenon in your own stock selections.

I am reminding you of this because, on occasion, we will all see businesses that are excelling, even though they are small in size. They are still under the radar of the investment analysts. These companies can have outsized growth year over year and may be excellent opportunities for investment. Even though they are small, their financials records are available to you by looking them up on MarketWatch, Barchart.com and/or Investors Business Daily (investors.com). These are companies for which the PEG ratio is more important than the P/E ratio. These are also companies that are sometimes targets of larger firms or venture capitalists who become aware of their potential.

If you invest only in very large corporations, you will be missing some great opportunities and you will be adopting some of the mentality of the investment funds that underperform the market 80% of the time. In your job, do you have a terrific supplier with a competitive edge that is publicly traded yet small? Is there a business in your neighborhood that is expanding rapidly and worthy of your analysis?

Another tip about smaller companies with excellent growth: They love talking about themselves. They may have an investor-relations specialist or someone in a similar role. When you speak with them on the phone, you will hear their excitement. Call them; they will be glad to talk to you. (What happens if you try to talk to investor relations at a mega-cap corporation? It's probably a waste of your time if you can even get someone on the phone).

You may not be able to fill your entire portfolio with small firms as described above, so you may well have some stock in proven companies that are larger. That's fine, and you should, but don't ignore the smaller fast growers that are still largely under the radar.

4.5 Sources of Investment Ideas

You will hear stock ideas from friends, CNBC, MSNBC, Yahoo Finance, and firms touting their paid recommendations like Zack's Investment Research, Motley Fool, and others. If you subscribe to Investors.com and/or their newspaper, IBD Weekly, you will have another source. Many sources like to discuss their past ideas that have worked out well. They rarely mention all of their recommendations that didn't work at all. So, you should think of these recommendations as candidates that you plan to evaluate using both fundamental analysis and technical analysis. One more source we will discuss later in this section: What Warren Buffett is holding in his Berkshire Hathaway portfolio.

4.5.1 Investors.com and IBD Weekly

We will start with these because you might well wish to subscribe to their website, investors.com, and also to their weekly newspaper, IBD Weekly. In case you are not familiar with IBD Weekly, it is quite different than the Wall Street Journal. The latter is a great newspaper, but IBD is for active investors and provides many valuable ideas and articles. IBD Weekly can be delivered to you almost anywhere in the U.S.

First a look at graphic always on the their webpage at investors.com. This is from July 8, 2025:

This graph replaced the prior one that described the market as one of three types:

      Market in Confirmed Uptrend

      Uptrend Under Pressure

      Market in Correction

The Stock Market Exposure is created by their models and may help you determine how much you should be invested.

Additionally there is always a table entitled Tech Leaders both on the website and in the print version (IBD Weekly):

Tech Leaders

Company	Symbol	Price	Comp Rtg	EPS Rtg	Rel Str	Annual EPS %Chg	LastQtr EPS %Chg
ACM Research	ACMR	19.24	99	99	99	+55	+118
Celestica	CLS	26.19	99	95	99	-13	+25
Eltek	ELTK	10.42	99	98	99	+100	+69
Nvidia	NVDA	421.96	99	93	99	+372	+429
Super Micro Comp	SMCI	285.03	99	95	99	+30	+34
Splunk	SPLK	148.01	99	82	98	+63	+689
Adobe	ADBE	557.87	99	97	97	-7.0	+20
CrowdStrike	CRWD	187.79	99	99	96	+129	+106

This table may be of interest to you if you like to include some tech stocks in your portfolio.

IBD is well known for its top 50 picks. They usually appear in the second section of the print edition. There are statistics and a graph of each stock. This is a great shopping list, but why not just buy all of them? Interestingly enough, IBD started an ETF of its top 50 stocks adjusted weekly to match the IBD 50 picks. Its symbol is FFTY. They may have regretted doing this. Here is a summary of how FFTY has performed through 10/18/23:

IBD® 50 ETF

ETF SUMMARY

The Innovator IBD® 50 ETF seeks to track the investment results of the IBD® 50 Index. IBD® 50 is Investor's Business Daily's signature investing tool—targeting companies that are generating outstanding profit growth, big sales increases, wide profit margins and a high return on equity.

GROWTH OF $10,000

Source: https://www.innovatoretfs.com/etf/?ticker=ffty

You can see at a glance that the performance is worse than dismal. The IBD 50 is a computer-generated list. But you had better think of it as a shopping list since FFTY performed so badly.

IBD is a great source, and their website is excellent for daily analysis of the markets. FFTY doesn't stop me from recommending it to you. One of the best features of their website is the analysis you can get of any stock if you are a subscriber. Let's look at the results when I type in F for Ford.

IBD STOCK CHECKUP®

Enter Stock Symbol/Company [GET STOCK CHECKUP]

Ford Motor (F)

COMPOSITE RATING | EPS RATING | RELATIVE STRENGTH RATING | SMR²RATING | ACC/DIS RATING³ |

RANK WITHIN AUTO MANUFACTURERS GROUP:

1	LI	LiAuto
2	RACE	Ferrari
3	STLA	Stellantis
4	TSLA	Tesla
7	F	Ford Motor

I entered F in the search box under 'Stock Checkup.' It shows a lot of information on the stock, including IBD's composite rating and a comparison with other stocks in the automotive industry.

This is a great tool that will provide you with stocks to consider that you may not be aware of.

Please spend some time getting familiar with IBD's website, investors.com and their print edition, IBD Weekly.

4.5.2 Subscription Research Services:

I have subscribed to three of the largest subscription services at various times. They have a few characteristics in common:

1) They all have special offers to encourage you to subscribe. Your subscription automatically renews if you don't cancel first, and the renewal rate is usually a lot higher than the rate you initially signed up for.

2) They all offer premium features for an extra cost, and some of the services are very aggressive about marketing them to you. One firm I used bombarded me constantly with emails and popups to the extent that I had to cut off all communications with them. (Their name starts with the last letter of the alphabet)

3) Subscription research services tell you about their past recommendations that were successful. They highlight those that have gone up by large percentages over the years. They typically do not tell you about their losers. Some present performance data, but you should look under the hood to see if it is objective.

4) The reviews on the web are worth considering for paid research firms like Motley Fool, Zacks, and Seeking Alpha. Consider looking at TrustPilot.com and Wallstreetzen.com. One warning on Zacks: they will barrage you with advertising once you contact them.

   Even for the firms that show graphs of stellar performance of their recommendations, you will see on these two websites reviews by people who lost serious money following their recommendations.

5) These services will occasionally email you about their latest recommendation. You will need to make your own assessment after consulting other sources.

6) I received a buy recommendation today for CPNG, Coupang Inc., a South Korean e-commerce firm. The accompanying article was quite detailed.

Their P/E ratio on Barchart.com is 74.29 ttm. Their yearly earnings for the year ending December 2023 are expected to be $0.31 per share. For the following year, they are projected to be $0.56/share. The stock price today is $17.69. Even if you use the estimated earnings for 2024 at $0.56/share, the P/E ratio would be 17.69/0.56=31.6. If you assume they will grow at a rate of 30% per year over the next 5 years, the PEG ratio would be 74.29/30=2.47. Here is a 5-year chart for CPNG as of 10/19/23:

Coupang Inc Cl A (CPNG)
17.69 +0.38 (+2.20%) 10/19/23 (NYSE)
17.60 x 5 17.68 x 1 POST-MARKET 17.60 -0.09 (-0.50%) 17:22 ET
SNAPSHOT CHART for Thu. Oct 19th, 2023
1-Day 5-Day 1-Mth 3-Mth 6-Mth 1-Yr 5-Yr 20-Yr
CPNG - Coupang Inc Cl A - Weekly OHLC Chart

You will need to decide if this is a good candidate for you. For me, the fundamentals may be okay, but the PEG ratio is high. The technical analysis tells me to wait until the chart shows strength to confirm the fundamentals. The one-year chart shows wide price swings. The service that recommended it has a 5-year view typically, and this stock may work well if you hold it for five years. Nonetheless, the ultimate decision is yours. Don't forget how FFTY has done, IBD's ETF of top 50 stocks.

4.5.3 Warren Buffet/ Berkshire Hathaway:

Warren Buffet, and his firm Berkshire Hathaway are so well known because they beat the averages consistently. He is a long-term investor and his firm does an excellent job of fundamental analysis of any stock or company they are considering. They are as good as it gets in assessing management performance, growth prospects, their competition or lack thereof, and the soundness of their balance sheet. Why am I including Berkshire Hathaway in my list of sources for investment ideas? For one, their holding are available for all to see. Every quarter, Berkshire Hathaway reports all of its stock holdings to the SEC in Form 13F. One place to access it is this link:

https://www.sec.gov/edgar/browse/?CIK=1067983.

Another is: https://13f.info/manager/0001067983-berkshire-hathaway-inc

Below is the first part of the 13F from the 13f.info source:

SYM	ISSUER NAME	CL	CUSIP	VALUE ($000)	%	SHARES
AAPL	APPLE INC	COM	037833100	177,591,247	51%	915,560,382
BAC	BANK AMER CORP	COM	060505104	29,632,524	8.5%	1,032,852,006
AXP	AMERICAN EXPRESS CO	COM	025816109	26,410,583	7.6%	151,610,700
KO	COCA COLA CO	COM	191216100	24,088,000	6.9%	400,000,000
CVX	CHEVRON CORP NEW	COM	166764100	19,372,950	5.6%	123,120,120
OXY	OCCIDENTAL PETE CORP	COM	674599105	13,178,796	3.8%	224,129,192
KHC	KRAFT HEINZ CO	COM	500754106	11,560,036	3.3%	325,634,818
MCO	MOODYS CORP	COM	615369105	8,578,175	2.5%	24,669,778
HPQ	HP INC	COM	48434L105	3,714,461	1.1%	120,952,818
DVA	DAVITA INC	COM	23918K108	3,626,521	1.0%	36,095,570
VRSN	VERISIGN INC	COM	92343E102	2,895,944	0.8%	12,815,613

Most of the stocks have been in their portfolio for a considerable length of time. They prefer to hold stocks for at least 5 years, and preferable much longer. Consequently, looking at the Berkshire Hathaway portfolio is certainly worth your time. This thought is possibly outside our topic of finding good stocks, but many of you are asking why not just buy Berkshire Hathaway?

Good question. If you wish to do so, there is nothing wrong with that. Their performance historically is excellent. I personally believe that buying BRK. makes a lot more sense than buying a mutual fund with all its fees and rules. Even so, you can still find stellar performers that can outperform even Berkshire Hathaway.

Are you concerned with Warren Buffett's age? He is 94 as of today, and his longtime partner, Charlie Munger, died recently at age 99. I hope Warren lives forever, but he won't. That said, you can take comfort in the fact that Berkshire has a good succession plan and their methods are well-established within the organization. Even after Warren Buffett is no longer at the helm, Berkshire Hathaway should continue its exceptional performance.

Don't miss the opportunity to dial in to Berkshire Hathaway's stockholders' meetings. Very informative, and you will get more timely information here on their recent purchases.

4.5.4 Financial Channels on Television (CNBC, Bloomberg, MSNBC):

These channels can provide valuable insights into individual companies and the broader market. They will keep you informed of upcoming economic data and they feature the results of Federal Open Market Committee meetings. They broadcast the Fed Chairman's speech following FOMC meetings, along with changes to the Fed Funds rate (if any).

All of this sounds very good. There are disadvantages to watching them consistently.

Here are two:

1) Interviews with CEOs can get you hyped about a company and induce you to make an investment without doing your detailed analysis.

2) The focus of the financial channels is often rather short-term. Yours should be long-term. Consequently, you may be led to make short-term decisions that you will regret later.

If you watch a financial channel, you may find candidate companies that you wish to investigate further. Your due diligence should include a look at Barchart.com and Investors.com. By now, you should be pretty structured in how to evaluate a company using technical analysis and fundamental analysis.

Section II
Strategies

Chapter 5: Strategies for Equities

I am very excited that you are beginning this section and this chapter. You will find methods here that give you guidance for filtering through the myriad of available stocks. You will see methods for timing your purchases. Most importantly, you will see discussions on risk management that are very important in minimizing losses. The industry in general, and managed funds in particular, are very poor at risk management. Protecting your capital is just as important as growing it.

5.1 Buy and Hold?

This brief question is of outsized importance and is worthy of our discussion here and your very serious consideration.

There are two primary schools of thought on this topic. The first is that staying fully invested in stocks produces a better long-term result than trying to "time" the market. This belief is in part supported by studies of strategies that attempt to time the market. These studies indicate that trend-following methods often result in late market exits during downturns and late returns to a fully invested position, thereby missing a significant portion of the early recovery period. Proponents of this school of thought may change their portfolios somewhat depending on the state of the economy, like being more in defensive stocks at times, such as utilities, but they are largely long stock at all times. There are some very successful investors who are proponents of this school of thought, including Warren Buffett.

The second school of thought is that one should be out of the market, partially or completely, during significant downturns to avoid painful losses that can and do occur. This school is closely aligned with the hedge fund industry, which comprises funds that have not only avoided severe losses but, in some cases, realized significant gains during down markets. Hedge funds vary in their strategies and use of derivatives, but it is common for them to utilize short positions and/or put options, especially in down markets. It is of great interest to older investors to determine whether and how they can avoid large downturns since their retirement funds are what they are counting on. Since the year 2000, there have been two bear markets with downturns of 49% and 56%. These are not events that retirement funds should experience. When an investor is in retirement, such losses can incur not only financial pain but severe stress and anxiety.

Now that you have read the preceding chapters of this book, you are prepared for a serious discussion of the merits and demerits of the two schools of thought. We will look at the four bear markets that have occurred since the year 2000 and determine whether a strategic investor could have done better than staying fully invested. Of course, one could say in hindsight that they would have been better off getting out of the market during these downturns, but we will look beyond that obvious statement to explore how they could have done so.

We will now look at the past four bear markets, 2000, 2007, 2020, and 2022 and consider what the strategic investor might have done. We will also present data that measures the performance of a portfolio that followed my methodology compared to one that remains fully invested. In each case, we will look at a weekly chart of the S&P 500 index with two moving averages (MAs), a 12-bar and a 30-bar. The 30-bar is fairly long since 30 weeks is equivalent to 150 days. We are using weekly charts because the time periods including and surrounding the bear markets are often 3 or more years long, and daily charts start looking pretty messy when they include over 2 years of data. We will also be looking at a chart of the Fed Fund Rate, which the

Federal Open Market Committee changes frequently. (See Chapter One on the Federal Reserve System). The Fed tends to drop the Fed Funds Rate whenever the economy is at risk of recession, and the chart indicates when recessions occurred.

After studying these four events, you will have a good understanding of methods to avoid serious downturns in the market.

First, the bear market started in the year 2000.

This was and is known as the dot-com bubble. A recession followed and included the 9/11 attacks of 2001. First, we will show the weekly chart as described in the paragraph above:

On this chart, the 12-bar moving average is Green, and the 30-bar Red. A 30-bar MA on a weekly chart is a good choice for showing longer-term trends in the market.

When Fed policy, a geopolitical event, or a health crisis indicates a heightened risk of a recession, the methodology I use is as follows:

Bear Market Methodology:

1) Exit the market when the slope of the 30-bar MA goes negative and when the 12-bar MA is below the 30-bar MA. The exit occurred on November 15, 2000.

2) Re-enter the market when the 30-Bar MA is again moving up and when the 12-bar MA is above the 30-bar MA. If the 30-bar MA is going down, and the 12-bar crosses above the 30-bar, do nothing. On this chart, you would re-enter your long positions on 5/15/2003. Yes, you would have been out of your long positions for over two years!

3) Some bear markets can be fast and short. If the signals above occur when the S&P index is already 15% or more from its recent high, do not exit the market; it's too late. This occurs rarely, but it did when Covid started in 2020, as we will see later.

Note from the chart above: If one thought that the criteria were met in the circle to re-enter the market, he/she would exit again very soon thereafter when it was clear that the long-term 30-bar MA was again showing a negative slope.

Implementation Notes: The charts and data are for the S&P 500 index and illustrate how the broader market behaves before and during bear markets. The behavior of a broad index is necessary to provide us with criteria for when to exit the market or at least significantly reduce our exposure. It also tells us when to re-enter the market. Most investors own individual stocks, and here are some key considerations for implementing this strategy. The methods are somewhat different for standard brokerage accounts and IRA accounts.

1) For IRA accounts

   In IRA accounts, there is no tax liability incurred by buying or selling; you are taxed only on the amounts withdrawn. So, when a bear market is imminent, sell most of your stock holdings. You may stay in cash, or you might consider buying a bond ETF. If after reading Chapter 1 on the FED and Chapter 6 on bond strategies and may have a sound opinion on the direction of interest rates. If so, consider TLT, a long bond fund, or TFX, an inverse bond fund.

2) For Standard (non-IRA) accounts

   If you have stocks that you are holding for long-term tax treatment, you may not wish to sell those and incur short-term gains. Sell your short-term investments and use part of those funds to buy SDS, an inverse S&P fund, or, if you have a margin account, sell short one of the broad market ETFs like SPY or QQQ. To protect yourself against losses on an individual stock, try to find another stock with which it is highly correlated and sell it. For example, if you have a long-term position in a home builder, you may keep it for tax reasons, but sell short a stock of a different builder. In a declining market, the short position should increase by the same amount that your long position decreases.

Next, let's also look at the chart of the Fed Funds Rate from year 2000 to 2023:

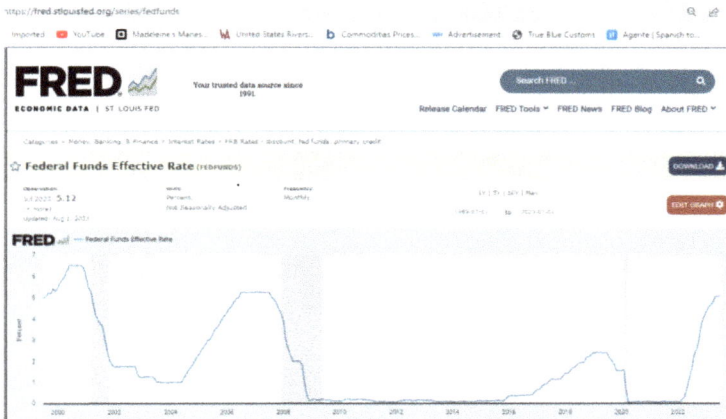

Above this graph is the link to the St. Louis Fed website from which it came. If you go to that link, you will see that you can edit the timeframe and other aspects of the graph. You can also download the data from which the graph was created if you wish. The graph shows not only the Fed Funds Rate but also the occurrence of recessions, which are indicated by shaded vertical stripes. This graph shows that the Fed began to drop the Fed Funds Rate in January of 2001. (To get this level of resolution, I downloaded the data). This is 2 months after our signal to exit the market, but it was confirmation that the Fed had major worries about an impending recession.

The methodology described exited the market when the S&P index was 1390 and re-entered when the index was at 950, thereby avoiding a loss of 440 points.

<u>Second, the bear market started in 2007. The bear market that started in 2007.</u>

This bear market is commonly known as the Housing Market Crash. It was preceded by low-interest mortgages offered with very low qualification standards. The stock market began to crumble as defaults on mortgages increased dramatically. A great read about some investors who got rich by anticipating these events is

"The Big Short" by Michael Lewis. A very entertaining and instructional book.

Below is the weekly graph of the S&P 500 index for this period of time. It shows the same MAs as in the earlier chart of the S&P Index:

Here again, the 12-bar MA is green, the 30-bar is Red. The methodology described above indicates an exit of long positions on January 1, 2008, and a re-entry on May 20, 2009. The S&P index was 1400 on exit and 940 on re-entry. We avoided a loss of 460 points!! Yes, you would have been out of the market for over a year!

Take another look at the Fed Funds chart above. The Fed started dropping the Fed Funds rate in August 2007. This was four months before our signal to exit the market, but it should have been a yellow flag to followers of the Fed. Note also from this chart the length of the ensuing recession. The Fed's action served as a warning, and the chart criteria of the bear market strategy provided the trigger to take action.

Third, The Bear Market of 2020

This bear market was caused by the beginning of the Covid pandemic. It was unanticipated by the Fed as it was unrelated to interest rates, inflation, or any other economic metric.

It was too quick for any trend following system to exit the market and our system couldn't react that quickly either. The chart below shows that our exit signal occurred when over a 15% drop had already taken place, and hence, per the 3 rules for our system, we did not take the signal. Some investors sold part of their holdings as soon as the Covid news showed that infections were growing rapidly not only in the U.S., but globally also. There is nothing wrong with concluding that the risks are too high, but mechanical systems were not of help here, including ours.

This is the chart of the market's reaction to Covid:

Fourth, The Bear Market of 2022

This bear market was in response to the Fed raising interest rates to combat inflation. As we said in Chapter 1 on the Federal Reserve System, they announced their intentions well in advance. You might wish to re-read section 1.6 of Chapter 1, The Federal Reserve System. This section indicated that the Fed communicated clearly starting in early 2022 that it would be raising interest rates to combat the problem of inflation far above its 2% target. They also stated in the press conferences that unemployment would rise and that GDP (Gross Domestic Product) would be impacted. The most common definition of recession is two quarters showing consecutive drops in GDP. We demonstrated in Section 1.6 how one can make considerable profits by anticipating that bond prices will fall as interest rates rise.

The conditions I mentioned above occurred as indicated by the blue arrow.

Using this methodology, one would exit the market at approximately 4250 on the S&P index, and reinvest when the shorter-term MA (green) crosses over the longer-term MA (red). This occurred at approximately 3975 on the S&P index. Having followed this methodology, one would have avoided the loss from 4250 to 3975, a loss of 275 points.

There is no drop in the Fed Funds rate to confirm this bear market; that's because the bear market was caused by the Fed raising interest rates substantially to combat inflation. As they predicted, there was a substantial increase in mortgage rates and a drop in estimates for GDP.

Limitations on the strategy I described in this section:

1) Exiting the market whenever the 30-bar MA turns negative and the 12-bar MA is below the 30-bar MA is best used when combined with economic factors. It is to be used when economic factors indicate a probable downturn. The dot-com bust and housing crisis were well publicized and reflected in FOMC press conferences. If you use it mechanically all the time over long periods, your portfolio will approximately duplicate the performance of the S&P 500 Index, but with many fewer serious downturns. It is not intended for that purpose. See Appendix A for more details on this.

2) The weekly charts are sufficient for most users to determine the signals for entries and exits. However, you can get finer resolution by using daily charts with 60-bar and 150-bar MAs. Since each bar on a weekly chart is 5 trading days, a 12-bar MA on a weekly chart is equivalent to a 60-bar MA on a daily chart, and a 30-bar MA on a weekly chart is equivalent to a 150 MA on a daily chart. For most of us, using the weekly charts is sufficient.

3) It is unlikely that an investor would liquidate 100% of his holding in one day and subsequently go long 100% upon a re-entry signal. Consequently, one might wish to reduce the results shown by approximately 10%.

Using the data for each of the 4 bear markets since the year 2000, the following table summarizes the results:

Bear Market	Years	Strategy Exit Date	$SPX at Exit	Strategy Re-Entry Date	$SPX at Re-Entry	$SPX Change Exit to Re-Entry
Dot Com	2000-2001	11/15/2000	1390	5/15/2001	950	-440
Housing Market	2007-2009	1/1/2008	1400	5/20/2009	940	-460
COVID 19	2020	N/A	N/A	N/A	N/A	0
Inflation Fight	2002	5/1/2022	4250	2/10/2023	3975	-275
				Total $SPX Points Saved by Strategy vs Long Position =		1175

Let's look at the net effect of using this bear market strategy from 11/15/2000 until 2/10/2023.

These are the dates of the first exit (dot-com) to the last re-entry (Inflation Fight).

The S&P index during this time increased from 1390 to 4250, representing a net gain of 2860 points.

The strategy saved 1175 points of losses, so the net gain is 2860+1175 = 4035 points. The difference is dramatic.

The results of using the bear market strategy are even larger than the above summary suggests. Large rallies often follow bear markets, and the user of the bear strategy has a larger balance following a bear market with which to participate. Let's assume there were two accounts that started just before the Dot Com bear market. Account A is fully invested at all times in an ETF that follows the $SPX index. (buy and hold)

Account B starts at the same time and uses the bear market strategy I described. Both accounts start with a balance of $100,000.

Let's see how the two accounts performed from the start of the Dot Com bear market to the end of the Inflation Fight:

Bear Market	Strategy Exit Date	$SPX at Exit	Strategy Re-Entry Date	$SPX at Re-Entry	$SPX Change: Exit to Re-Entry	% Change (Bear Market)	%Change Between Bear Mkt	Balance Acct A	Balance Acct B
								$100,000	$100,000
Dot Com	11/15/2000	1390	5/15/2001	950	-440	-31.65%		$68,350	$100,000
Interim Between Bear Markets (5/15/2001-1/1/2008)							47.3?%	$100,727	$147,370
Housing Market	1/1/2008	1400	5/20/2009	940	-460	-32.86%		$67,628	$147,370
Interim Between Bear Markets (5/20/2009-5/1/2022)							352.13%	$305,787	$666,304
Inflation Fight	5/1/2022	4250	2/10/2023	3975	-275	-6.47%		$305,766	$666,304

Look at the last two columns summarizing the two accounts. Don't hurry over this; it is important. You can verify the % data and account balances using the data from the earlier table showing the 4 bear markets since the year 2000.

Account A above is fully invested in an ETF such as SPY, which tracks the S&P 500 index. Account B is also invested in a similar ETF, and hence, the account holder can enter and exit the market very rapidly at will. The average investor may be invested in a collection of individual issues, however, exiting the market and re-entering is a bit more involved in that multiple trades are required. That is why on the last page, I recommended de-rating the results by 10% or so to account for the extra time to reposition the account. Making that assumption, the last figure in the oval above might be more like $666,304 x 90% = $599,673. A 10% reduction is likely more than necessary, and you can make your own estimate. This paragraph is to assure the reader that the described methodology is executable and can produce results as indicated.

Just as important: There was great stress and angst among buy-and-hold investors who rode the roller coaster market of the last few years. Avoiding serious downturns enables lower stress and a feeling of being more in control.

Let's think about this from the 20,000-foot level. In 2022, the Fed essentially said that interest rates would rise substantially. When asked if the stock market would suffer, Chairman Powell stated that the economy would slow as a result. Did a thinking investor just sit there and watch his stocks drop by 25.4% I don't think so. Similarly, in 2007, the dire straits of the economy were well publicized and the Fed dropped the Fed Funds rate to zero. Did it make sense to just ride it out and take your lumps? NO.

Some of the most respected investment firms took a hit during these bear markets. Below is a chart of the performance of 4 of Morgan Stanley's largest funds. Look at the one-year performance that ended in March 2023. This period includes most of the 2022 bear market.

These results are truly dismal. See for yourself.

Funds			Average Annual Total Returns		
INDEX: Hide Display	PEER GROUPS: Hide Display		SALES CHARGE': At NAV Maximum		
FUND NAME ▲	SHARE CLASS ▲	AS OF DATE ▾	YTD ▾	1 YR ▾	
MPAIX Advantage Portfolio	I	03/31/2023	19.26	-27.72	
MSBVX American Resilience Portfolio	I	03/31/2023	5.47	--	
MPEGX Discovery Portfolio	I	03/31/2023	16.75	-40.39	
MAAQX Dynamic Value Portfolio	I	03/31/2023	-2.89	-6.76	
MSEQX Growth Portfolio	I	03/31/2023	17.56	-36.37	
MSSGX Inception Portfolio	I	03/31/2023	21.03	-33.39	

By now, you know what my position is on whether to stay fully invested or not. Proponents of the buy-and-hold philosophy occasionally ridicule efforts to beat the S&P by trying to "time the market". I hope that I have convinced you that buy-and-hold is the easiest strategy; however, it doesn't make sense at times when you have a body of evidence that markets are going lower.

Additional context for the considerations of this section:

There are many firms in the U.S, primarily in New York, that specialize in trend-following strategies. These methods are primarily used in managing hedge funds and accounts of large institutional investors.. The goals are often to invest in futures and/or other derivatives whose underlying assets are not highly correlated to U.S. equities. For example, a trend-following fund might be long copper futures and short oil futures if both were showing movement that met their criteria for a trend. Individuals can participate if they satisfy at least one of the following criteria to be a "qualified investor".

1) Their income has been above $200,000 per year for each of the last two years, or above $300,000 if they file jointly with a spouse

2) Their net worth, exclusive of their primary residence, exceeds $1 million.

3) They are also expected to have a certain level of familiarity with the derivatives used by the hedge fund or by the manager of a private fund.

The trend-following sector of the investment world is quite large. At the end of 2021, it was estimated to exceed $300 billion. This is a very large sector, yet many investors are unfamiliar with it since it is not commonly covered by the financial press, nor do commercial brokerages usually publicize it.

Why am I mentioning this sector of investments here? Because this sector specializes in identifying when trends start and when they end and trends can be either up or down in the markets in which they participate. Trend-following funds are totally agnostic as to whether a trend is up or down. The discussion in this section of The Strategic Investor, speaking of times when it is likely that the equity markets will be entering bear market territory, is a subset of the everyday thought processes of trend-following funds. If you have decided that religious adherence to buy and hold isn't for you, take comfort in the fact that a large sector of the markets, the trend-following funds, shares your thought processes.

5.2 Allocation to Stocks – What % Should You Be Invested?

This is a very important consideration. If you are only 50% invested in stocks in a strong up market, your chance of beating the S&P 500 index is very slim. I am keenly aware of this risk, because there have been times when I held back too much, i.e., I had too much in cash. The previous section, 5.1 Buy and Hold? gave you guidelines for exiting the market during serious downturns. This should help you in know that the rest of the time, you should be invested at least 80%. Keep in mind that if you are competing with the S&P 500 index, your competitor is always 100% invested by definition.

In section 5.1, we spoke of using a weekly chart of the S&P 500 index with two moving averages superimposed, a 12-bar MA and a 30-Bar MA. Below is a 5-year chart with these two MAs:

You should be almost 100% long stocks when the 12-bar MA (green) is above the 30-bar MA (red).

In addition to the guidelines above, you might reference the Investor Business Daily overall market assessment that we described in section 4.5.1:

Stock Market Exposure

0-20%   20-40%   40-60%   60-80%   80-100%

40% to 60% Invested

This is an example of what you will see:

To access the IBD recommendation, go to Investors.com and hover your mouse over Market Trend near the top of the page. A drop-down list appears. Select <u>ETF Market Strategy</u>. You will see a graphic like the one above.

IBD recommendations may differ from the guidelines I provided, but having two recommendations to guide you is beneficial. Their model doesn't include the important seasonality considerations that you will see below, so let them supersede IBD during the critical times. Also, please let my guidelines on ducking bear markets take precedence over IBD recommendations when these important down markets appear.

5.2.1 Seasonality

There are times of the year that have strong seasonal tendencies. Let's look at the monthly performance of the S&P 500 index using data from the past 50 years. The following chart is from capital.com at the following link:

https://capital.com/stock-market-seasonal-trends-when-is-the-best-and-worst-time-to-invest-in-stocks

	1	2	3	4	5	6	7	8	9	10	11	12
S&P 500	1.0%	0.1%	0.9%	1.6%	0.7%	0.3%	0.9%	0.0%	-0.8%	0.9%	1.4%	1.3%

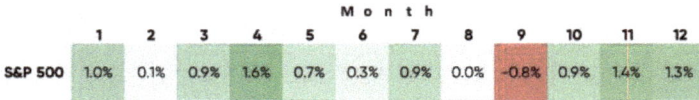

November, December, and January are strong seasonally. Take advantage of this trend.

September is horrible and the September swoon often drifts into the early parts of October. During the three strong months of November, December, and January be 100% long if either criterion above is positive: the IBD market assessment = Confirmed Uptrend or the 12 bar MA on the weekly chart of $SPX being above the 30 bar MA. This exception to what we said a few paragraphs earlier about using two criteria only holds during these three months.

5.2.2 Is Age a Factor In Allocation to Stocks?

This question has been discussed at least as far back as the stock market meltdown in 1929. There are proponents of the approach that, as one gets close to or into retirement that they should take less risk and allocate more funds into bonds. There are "Age Related Funds" that use a formula to implement this approach. One of the most common approaches suggests that you should allocate a percentage of your investment capital to bonds based on your age. Some of these funds, for example, would recommend that a 70 year old person should be 70% in bonds

Chapter 1 on the Federal Reserve System, Chapter 2, Bond Basics, and Chapter 3, Charts and Technical Analysis, gave you a very good understanding on how bonds vary with interest rates, how the Fed gives us guidance on the future of interest rates, and how technical analysis can help us decide if and when to buy bond funds. We looked in section 2.5 (Chapter 2) to see how bonds fell dramatically in 2022 as interest rates rose, and concluded (correctly) that bonds are not without risk. Yes, there are times to own bonds, but if you owned TLT in 2022, the bond ETF of 20-year+ treasuries, and had a significant allocation to bonds, you suffered greatly. Your level of understanding of bonds should allow you to know when to hold them and whether longer-dated bonds are for you, considering their higher sensitivity to interest rate changes.

It is worth looking at the comparative performance of stocks vs bonds over time. For the period from 1926 to 2019, an investment in bonds yielded an average annual return of 5.3%. For the same period of time, an investment in stocks produced an average annual return of 10.3%.

Over the past decade, the S&P index has experienced an average annual increase of 12.39%.[15]

Approaches that suggest that older investors should be heavily invested in bonds have two major drawbacks; 1) poor returns over time and 2) downturns such as 2022. The only way a bond investor can avoid downturns is to invest only in short dated bonds, 5 years or less, but the returns there are very low. The motivation to be heavily in bonds is to avoid stock market risk, but we have shown you how to avoid major drawdowns earlier in this chapter. The discussion above is in the context of the question about allocation to stocks as an older, more risk averse investor. Rather than being heavily in bonds, older investors should consider stocks with high dividends, (value stocks), avoiding stocks with high P/E ratios, and keeping whatever % of their capital they think is appropriate in CDs, or very short-term bond funds such as SGOV.

---

[15] Source: https://www.businessinsider.com/

5.3 Thematic Investing

Thematic investing is the process of identifying and investing in dominant trends in the economy, sometimes called Megatrends. Examples of recent and current themes are Artificial Intelligence, Robotics and Automation, Green Energy, Semiconductors, and ESG (environmental, social, and governance). Interest in thematic investments has more than tripled since the COVID pandemic started. [16]

Themes are used by investors to focus on areas of the market they believe will outperform the averages. They are also used by some to identify stocks that are consistent with their values or interests. This latter use can be morally and ethically satisfying but may lead to investments that to not perform as well as the averages.

In response to the increased interest in thematic investing, many ETFs have been created that offer focused exposure to some of the more common themes. Here's a few examples:

- SMH: VanEck Semiconductor ETF
- BOTZ: GE Robotics and AI ETF
- ARKK: ARK Innovation ETF (disruptive innovation)
- CIBR: First Trust NASDAQ Cybersecurity ETF

ETFs for thematic investors have the advantage that they do a lot of the analysis of stocks in the area of interest and provide a degree of diversification within the area.

There are brokerages who offer products for thematic investors. Charles Schwab offers lists of stock by theme and the ability for

---

[16] Source: 'Thematic investing' has taken off. How to capitalize on trends (cnbc.com)

the client to add or delete stocks from any theme list, and invest in the tailored list of stocks.

There is a lot of press and possibly a little hype about thematic investments so, in fairness, I will include here some cautionary thoughts. The following is an excerpt from an article by Adam Shell in Investor Business Daily on 11/16/23:

"Still, as with any investment, specific themes that hold baskets of stocks aren't guaranteed to beat the market. They usually lag. In fact, so-called theme funds tracked by Morningstar delivered annualized total returns of 7.2% vs. a 10.6% return for Morningstar's U.S. Market Index from January 2017 (when enough theme funds existed to merit computing an average return) to April 2023, according to Morningstar's John Rekenthaler in a story published in June, titled "Thematic Investing: Just Say No."

You might wish to look at an article by Morningstar on Theme ETFs:

Despite Recent Struggles, Thematic Funds Are Here to Stay | Morningstar

https://www.morningstar.com/funds/despite-recent-struggles-thematic-funds-are-here-stay

Here is a graphic from that article on how some of the popular theme ETFs have performed over the past 5 years:

Best and Worst Theme Performance, Trailing 5 Years

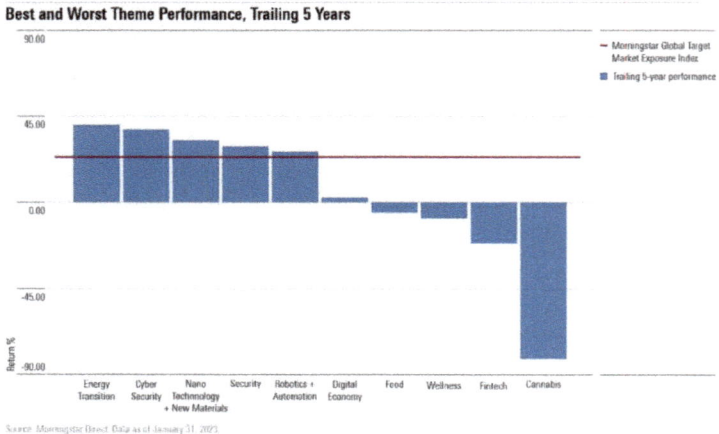

— Morningstar Global Target Market Exposure Index
▪ Trailing 5-year performance

Source: Morningstar Direct. Data as of January 31, 2023.

Also from this article, the following excerpt is worthy of note:

"This data suggests that if you picked a thematic fund at random, your chances of that fund surviving and outperforming the global equity market never rose above 50% over any of the time periods highlighted. This is why it's so important to have a robust framework for assessing these funds."

How to resolve the disparity between the brokerages' enthusiasm for thematics and the many new thematic ETFs with the paragraph above? After all, Morningstar is a reliable, objective source. Here's my take on that:

- Brokerages like to sell what the public is interested in and they are heavily marketing theme funds. Marketing material is not always objective.

- Morningstar's conclusions are based upon a large set of theme funds. There aren't that many viable themes that will last over time.

- There have been themes with funds focused on them that have performed well.

- Some themes have had obvious risks and should be avoided.

- Investing in themes can be successful, but the data suggests caution.

Here are a few criteria to consider before buying a theme fund:

1. Evidence that the trend will continue for at least 5 years.

2. Opinions by economists that confirm this trend is solid.

3. Does IBD, Motley Fool, or Seeking Alpha give good ratings to the top 4 or 5 stocks in the fund? (When you enter fund symbol into Barchart.com, you will see a link on the left, down a bit for "constituents". Selecting "constituents will show you a list of the holdings of the fund.

5.4 Allocation Between Growth and Value Stocks

You will hear a lot in the financial press about which category is better at any point in time, but allow me to give you some data to help quantify the performance of both categories in different market conditions. There definitely are times when you should be largely in value stocks, and other times when you should be in growth stocks. The S&P index can't change the allocation much, but you can, and this gives you an advantage.

Let's start with a definition of what a growth stock is and what a value stock is.

Value Stock: A value stock is characterized by a low P/E ratio and has an established income stream not subject to large risk. By a low P/E ratio, I mean below that of the S&P 500 index. Value stocks are also often good dividend payers. They are companies with manageable or low debt levels. They are relatively stable in all markets.

Charlie Munger, the late partner of Warren Buffett, made the following statement regarding the investing philosophy of Ben Graham, whom Charlie admired:

"Graham's investment philosophy focused on identifying undervalued securities through fundamental analysis. His approach wasn't about acquiring cheap companies; it involved understanding a company's intrinsic value, separate from its market price. Graham emphasized thorough financial scrutiny, seeking firms with strong balance sheets, minimal debt, and strong cash flows — aspects that the market frequently ignores."[17]

Growth Stock: A growth stock has a P/E ratio significantly higher than that of the S&P 500 index. They have an annual growth of 20% or more per year. They may be in fast-changing markets such as technology. Their PEG ratio is important to look at to put their high P/E ratio in context.

This year, prominent growth stocks have been Amazon, Meta, Nvidia, AMD, and Microsoft.

Now that we have the terms defined, let's look at how each category has fared in different market conditions. We will look at two graphs next, one for value stocks and one for growth stocks. Each graph is for the last ten years.

First, the value stocks: IVE is the ETF, and the graph is from Barchart.com

---

[17] source: https://www.yahoo.com/finance/news/charlie-mungers-final-advice-investors-175312388.html

S&P 500 Value Ishares ETF (IVE)

Next for growth stocks. The ETF for growth stocks has the ticker symbol IVE. The graph is again from Barchart.com

S&P 500 Growth Ishares ETF (IVW)

Let's look at the comparative performance in a bull market and a bear market:

1) The first recession started in 2020 when COVID struck. From the beginning of the graphs in 2013 until the start of the recession, these were the comparative results:

   Value stocks went from an index value of 90.3 to 132.1 (Up 46.3%)

   Growth stock went from an index value of 26.0 to 52.8 (Up 103.1%)

   Yes, Growth stocks outperform in strong up markets.

2) In the bear market of 2022, here were the comparative results:

Value stocks went from a high of 160.4to a low of 127.3. (Down 20.6%)

Growth stock went from a high of 85.1 to a low of 55.3. (Down 35.0%)

In keeping with what we said in section 5.2, growth stocks are fine when either or both of the conditions are in place to be 100% invested. Since grown stocks are subject to larger corrections, don't be heavily invested in them otherwise.

5.5 Evaluating Candidate Stocks for Your Portfolio

In Chapter 4, paragraph 4.5, we discussed some excellent sources for identifying stocks that may be of interest to you. That is, stocks that you may wish to be invested in. The top 3 were Investors Business Daily, subscription research services, and Berkshire Hathaway's portfolio.

Then, in section 5.4 in this chapter, we gave some guidelines on when to emphasize growth stocks and when to be heavier in value stocks. In our present section, I would like to suggest guidelines for stock selection from your list of candidates. The methodology is somewhat different for value stocks and growth stocks, so let's discuss them separately.

5.5.1. Evaluating Value Stocks

I am going to suggest a list of criteria. A yes decision by you to invest should be made only if most of these criteria are satisfied.

1. P/E ratio is less than that of the S&P Index
2. All of the past 5 years were profitable
3. The company has control over prices. (not too much competition)

4. Business model based on repeat business
5. Share price above $10.00
6. Earnings growth above 10% per year (past 5 years and projected 3 to 5 years)
7. Stable management

In addition to the above, if you are a subscriber to investors.com, do a stock checkup. The overall score should be 80% or higher.

It is worth noting that Peter Lynch loves companies that have a niche to themselves. An example would be a company that owns a rock quarry in an area of the country where construction is underway. It is very unlikely that someone else would start a rock quarry nearby. It is also unlikely that analysts are following the company even though it is publicly traded. Peter likes stocks in boring industries and is largely under the radar. Often, they are underpriced.

Since we recommended looking at Berkshire Hathaway's portfolio for great ideas, it is worth mentioning that although Warren Buffett is known as a value investor, not all of Berkshire's stock holdings are value stocks by the definition above or by most definitions of value stocks, including that of Investopedia. Apple is a good example and is Berkshire Hathaway's largest holding. That said, their portfolio is great for shopping. Yes, most of his stocks are in the value category.

5.5.2 Evaluating Growth Stocks

You will see some differences here from above:
1. P/E ratio is higher than that of the S&P Index
2. The PEG ratio is 2.0 or less
3. All of the past 3 years were profitable
4. There is clearly a growing market for their products

5. Business model based on innovation

6. Share price above $10.00

7. Earnings growth above 10% per year (past 3 years)

8. Earnings growth projection is above 15% per year for the next 3 to 5 years

9. Stable management

It is worth noting that David and Tom Gardner, founders of The Motley Fool, don't mind buying stocks with high P/E ratios. Here's an excerpt from The Motley Fool Investment Guide on page 153:

"In more than twenty years of picking stocks, going way back to the early days

of Motley Fool, many of our best-performing stocks were considered "grossly overvalued when we recommended them to our readers."

A note on buying high P/E stocks: The price swings are wider, so make sure you are prepared.

One resource I use in evaluating growth stocks is the finance.yahoo.com website. When you enter the ticker symbol of your candidate stock and then select Analysis from the horizontal list of choices below, after scrolling down, you will see an estimate of the growth rate over the next five years. It should be above 15% to be exciting as a growth stock.

5.6 Timing Your Purchase

In section 5.1, we defined when to be out of the stock market entirely. We also said that you should be long the market when looking at the weekly chart of the S&P500 Index ($SPX), and the 12-bar moving average is above the 30-bar moving average. Another signal to be long the market is when Investor's Business Daily considers the market direction to be a Confirmed Uptrend.

These should be prerequisites for stock purchases. One is sufficient; two is compelling.

In addition to the above criteria based on the broader market, you should buy into strength on the weekly or daily chart of the stock you have chosen. Let's look at the following weekly chart of Microsoft:

This is a weekly chart with a 20-bar Moving Average in red. Given your long-term focus, similar to Warren Buffett, Motley Fool, and Peter Lynch, it's sensible to utilize the weekly chart, which displays a 5-year history. Please consider making your new commitment to a stock only when the 20-bar MA is on the rise. Yes, when you get excited about a stock, you will want to buy it now, but please wait for the technicals to agree.

Once this criterion is reached, I also look at the daily chart. I buy only when the 9-bar moving average is rising also. This last step will give you an additional edge. See how the daily view can help you pick an excellent entry point:

Microsoft Corp (MSFT)
370.92 +2.12 (+0.57%) 14:12 ET (NASDAQ)
370.87 x 100 370.92 x 200 REALTIME by CBoe (BZX)
SNAPSHOT CHART for Thu, Dec 7th, 2023

In summary, look at the technical indicators for the broader market first. If they are satisfied, and your analysis of a particular stock is telling you to invest, time your entry by using charts of the stock with a 20-bar MA on the weekly chart and a 9-bar MA on the daily chart.

In the next section, we will look at how to minimize losses. Yes, you will have some, but the object of the game is not ever to have a losing position; it is to have few of them and to limit any losses so that they do not seriously impact the value of your portfolio.

5.7 Risk Management for Individual Stocks

We discussed in section 5.1 (Buy and Hold?) how important it is to sit out most bear markets. Proper risk management is important and will give you a substantial edge over the average investor. The mutual funds are very poor at it, as we illustrated with the losses incurred in those run by Morgan Stanley in 2022. Most financial advisors are equally inept at risk management.

To outperform mutual funds, one of the most effective strategies is to excel at risk management.

Let's first look at a two-year weekly chart of Rockwell Automation.

Rockwell Automation Inc (ROK)
299.52 -5.07 (-1.66%) 1:40 ET [NYSE]
299.52 x 7   299.81 x 7   REALTIME by Cboe BZX)
SNAPSHOT CHART for Tue, Jan 16th, 2024
ROK - Rockwell Automation Inc - Weekly OHLC Chart

This stock was on many analysts' buy lists, partly because of the auto industry moving to increase the use of robotics. You might very well have bought it in November 2022 when the 20-bar MA was positive.

The high was $348. On July 18, 2023, the price on 10/25/23, just three months later, was $263.

This can happen even to highly rated stocks. This drop from the high was 24.4%.

The losses this year were also severe for Ulta Beauty, Inc. Let look at a two-year weekly chart:

Ulta Beauty Inc (ULTA)
481.20 -0.88 (-0.18%) 1:44 ET [NASDAQ]
480.85 x 3   481.37 x 5   REALTIME by Cboe BZX)
SNAPSHOT CHART for Tue, Jan 16th, 2024
ULTA - Ulta Beauty Inc - Weekly OHLC Chart

The high in April 2023 was $557. On October 25, 2023, the price was $378.

This loss of 31.5% was also painful.

Please note that the two examples here, ROK and ULTA, show losses during times when the stock market was doing fairly well. The S&P Index was higher in October 2023 than it was in February.

5.7.1 Methods to Limit Your Risk

Here are three, and you should use at least one of them.

1. <u>Fixed percentage stop loss</u>

   This method has you sell a stock that is a certain percentage off its high during the last 6 months. I often use 8% or 10%.Before choosing the percentage, look at a graph of the stock. Different stocks have different volatilities, i.e., the amount of variation they experience. Pick a percentage that doesn't take you out prematurely.

   Take another look at the two charts above. A 10% or 8% stop would have avoided the bulk of the losses. Does this mean that you have given up on this stock forever?

   No, but for you to buy it again, it would have to satisfy the criteria for its initial purchase. It should have the 20-bar MA on the weekly chart clearly going up.

   You can implement this using a Trailing Stop order. You can specify either the % or price change in dollars. If the stock price drops to the specified level, it will be sold. The great thing about trailing stops is that if your stock goes up, the trailing stop price moves up by the same amount.

2. Moving Averages Crossover Exit (weekly chart)

    This method requires you to sell your position in a stock if the 6-bar MA on the weekly chart crosses under the 20-bar MA. Let's look at a weekly chart of ULTA to see when this criterion would have told you to sell.

    This methodology would have you sell at $490, which would have you incur a larger loss than using a fixed percentage stop.

    You will notice from the chart above that the 6-bar and 20-bar MAs crossed numerous times during the flatter part of the chart in early 2022. This crossover exit works best after a notable increase in price.

3) 9 Bar moving average on the daily chart

    You might recall this is also used as a criterion for entering new positions. With this exit, you sell when the 9-bar MA begins to slope downward. This exit will get triggered more often than #2 above, but is useful especially if your time frame is shorter, i.e., months, not years.

There is another risk mitigation strategy, but it is out of the scope of this book. Nonetheless, interest readers may wish to read further on this. I am talking about selling out of the money calls against stocks that you own. You may even be able to do this multiple times on the same stock if there is a mild decline occurring. This technique allows you to keep a stock for long-term gains without having to sell it before the time frame is satisfied.

5.8 An Illustrative Example (referencing many points from this chapter)

This example is real in the sense that I have it in my portfolio.

5.8.1 Background

Artificial Intelligence has been a very important development that appears to have the potential to add value to many industries. It will increase the capability of search engines, diagnostics in medicine, optimization of shipping routes and schedules, and even the design of computer chips. Nvidia uses AI to help design its high-power chips. AI is a great example of a theme, and is one of the most important themes to appear on the horizon in many years.

AI will require increased horsepower in computing. Data centers will be a growth segment due to AI, as cloud computing is now performed there more than it was previously, when computing was done locally. The best plays on AI seem to be in chip designers like Nvidia and AMD, and in software companies like Microsoft that enable the use of AI. Microsoft has its own AI products, CoPilot and Azure, and is investing heavily in new AI tools and support software.

I saw an investment opportunity here that seemed compelling. I decided to invest in Microsoft. It is not an ETF, but it does satisfy the criteria for thematic funds stated in section 5.3.

Let's look at the weekly and daily charts of Microsoft. First the weekly chart with 6-bar and 20-bar moving averages:

Microsoft Corp (MSFT)

Our criteria for being long the broad market are outlined in section 5: The 12-bar MA is above the 30-bar MA on the weekly chart of the S&P 500 index. This kept us out of the market in general for most of 2022.

Our criteria to buy an individual stock are for the 6-Bar MA to be above the 20-bar MA on its weekly chart. You can see from the chart above that this criterion was satisfied in February of 2023. If you bought MSFT at that time, and the criterion you use to exit a position (section 5.7.1) took you out in September of 2023, you would have rebought MSFT in early November when the 6-bar MA was again above the 12-bar MA.

Using the criteria and methods above, you would have bought MSFT at approximately $250.00 per share and still own it now that the share price is $406. This gain has been realized in less than 18 months!

As the title of this section states, our example illustrates many points from this chapter:

- We used the logic of Themes to select the AI segment of the market.
- We satisfied the criteria for a good Theme in section 5.3.

- We used our criteria to be in the broader market.

- We used Technical Analysis to define our entry point for MSFT.

I believe that MSFT will meet or exceed growth targets of 15% or more per year for the next 5 years. That said, if the market goes through a serious downturn, I am confident that you now have excellent criteria on when to be out of the market and when to exit a stock position.

Chapter 6: Strategies for Bonds

Historically, bonds have been considered a safe haven with certain income and low risk. Many investment managers routinely put higher percentages of clients' money in bonds as their age increases. It was popular to use as a guideline, using your age as the percentage of your money to put in bonds rather than stocks. The logic here was that a person in their retirement years should not be taking very much risk, and hence, bonds were a better investment for them.

Some of these approaches have been very unsuccessful, especially in periods of rising interest rates. The financial industry has been way too slow in evolving its approach to bonds, and the investing public has suffered because of it. In this chapter, after a brief review of the relationship between bond prices and interest rates, we will look at how the banks have suffered by not managing their bond portfolios properly, and also how some respected managed funds have done the same. Then we will look at strategies for you, the individual investor.

6.1 A Brief Review - Bond Basics

In Chapter 2, Bond Basics, we discussed how bond prices drop when interest rates rise and increase when interest rates drop. The logic is pretty straightforward. Possibly you own a 20-year bond paying 3% interest. If interest rates rise, and new 20-year bonds are now paying 3.5 %, your bond is no longer competitive, so its price will fall.

You may wish to review Chapter 2, as it contains a lot of information about bond pricing and price risk. In addition to the basic relationship of bond prices and interest rates we discussed how longer duration bonds are much more sensitive to changes in interest rates than shorter duration bonds.

For review, here is an excerpt from Chapter 2 where we used a bond calculator to see the price sensitivity of a 20-year bond to a 1% change in interest rates:

Yield To Maturity	Market Price

Bond Face Value/Par Value ($)

1000

Years to Maturity

20

Annual Coupon Rate (%)

1.5

Yield to Maturity (Market Yield) (%)

6.5

Coupon Payment Frequency

○ Monthly
○ Quarterly
○ Annually

● Twice a Year
○ None (Zero Coupon)

Calculate **Clear**

Results

Current Market Price ($) = 444.79

Macaulay Bond Duration = 15.6 Years

Modified Bond Duration (Δ%/1%) = 15.08

Now, if interest rates increase by 1% (from 6.5% to 7.5%), the bond price will drop by 15.08% Yikes! In 2022, interest rates rose dramatically, and long bonds dropped greatly. Banks typically hold large amounts of U.S. treasuries, often long-duration bonds.

The bond calculator we used was from this link:

https://www.mymathtables.com/calculator/finance/bond-duration-calculator.html

6.2 Losses by Banks and Pension Funds

The industry has been so backward in its thinking about bonds and bond risks that the reserves of many banks in the United States shrank dangerously in 2022 as the Fed raised the Fed Funds rate from near zero to almost 5%. The Fed announced its intention to raise rates well in advance. The banks should have anticipated that their long-dated treasuries would decline in value, yet many banks took no action other than to suffer the consequences.

During 2022, the Fed raised the Fed Funds rate from zero to 4%. See the following graph:

These changes were made by the Federal Open Market Committee.

Naturally, the rates of all bonds rose correspondingly. The following graph shows the rate changes during 2022 of the U.S. 20-year treasury bond:

Market Yield on U.S. Treasury Securities at 20-Year Constant Maturity, Quoted on an Investment Basis (DGS20)

During 2022, the interest rate on the U.S. 20-year bond went from 2% to 4%!

Look what happened to the bond ETF, TLT. (20+year maturity bonds)

During 2022, the TLT ETF went from $142.00 to $84.00. The idea that bonds are a great safe haven in a down stock market got buried in 2022.

The Fed was very clear about its intentions to raise interest rates substantially in 2022 to fight inflation. See paragraph 1.6 of Chapter 1, The Federal Reserve System.

In 2022, some banks saw their reserves plummet as the value of their bond portfolios shrank.

Silicon Valley Bank was one of the first. It collapsed the bank.

Note the paragraph below from CNN on the collapse of Silicon Valley Bank:[18]

Why did it collapse?

SVB's collapse came suddenly, following a frenetic 48 hours during which customers yanked deposits from the lender in a classic run on the bank.

But the root of its demise goes back several years. Like many other banks, SVB ploughed billions into US government bonds during the era of near-zero interest rates.

What seemed like a safe bet quickly came unstuck, as the Federal Reserve hiked interest rates aggressively to tame inflation.

Could the bank have minimized its losses? Obviously, they could have shifted their bonds to notes with very short duration or just sold them and kept the cash on their balance sheet.

Unfortunately, many other banks, especially regional banks, suffered huge losses also, but fortunately, most of them survived.

See the article at this link:

https://www.latimes.com/business/story/2022-07-20/calpers-reports-first-loss-for-pension-fund-since-great-recession

California pension fund reports first loss since Great Recession - Los Angeles Times (latimes.com)

Pension funds were hurt significantly in 2022, as were the banks mentioned in section 6.1.

---

[18] source: Why Silicon Valley Bank collapsed and what it could mean | CNN Business   March 13, 2023

The following is a quote from an article in the Los Angeles Times on September 29, 2022:[19]

"In California, the cumulative assets of 18 of the largest pension funds are expected to drop this year from $1.37 trillion to $1.09 trillion, lowering the funding ratio from 86.8% to 79.6%, according to an update of Equable's annual report on the state of pensions, titled "The Era of Volatility: Asset Shocks, Inflation and War." A pension fund's ideal target is full funding, or a 100% ratio, which the plans last reached cumulatively in 2007, just before the financial crisis."

The pension funds are run by experienced managers that had more latitude than the banks. The pension funds don't have the same reserve requirements as the banks, and are not obligated to own any long-term government bonds at all. The point is that even the most experienced fund managers were caught off guard in 2022, and the results were painful. The pain and suffering are only exacerbated by the fact that the Fed announced its intentions to raise interest rates materially during 2022, and as a consequence, fund managers could have known with certainty that long-term bonds would sink in value.

I am emphasizing the losses incurred in bonds to underscore the reality that you must not just put investment dollars, and particularly retirement assets, into bonds on the assumption that bonds are safe and you can't get hurt owning bonds.

https://equable.org/state-of-pensions-2022/

6.3 When Should You Own Bonds?

In section 5.2 of Chapter 2, there is the following paragraph that compares the long-term performance of bonds vs stocks:

---

[19] Source: https://www.latimes.com/business/story/2022-09-29/are-calpers-calstrs-other-pension-plans-headed-for-crisis

"It is worth looking at the comparative performance of stocks vs bonds over time. For the time period of 1926 to 2019, an investment in bonds produced an average annual return of 5.3%. For the same period of time, an investment in stocks produced an average annual return of 10.3%.

For the past 10 years, the S&P index has had an average annual increase of 12.39%.[20]

It is pretty clear that bonds underperform stocks most of the time. There are three times when this is not the case:

1) When the stock market is in a bear market. During most serious downturns, almost anything outperforms the averages, including cash, CDs, and bonds. In section 5.1, we discussed when and how to avoid a bear market in stocks. During bear markets, it may be advisable to hold bonds if interest rates are not rising, which would cause bond prices to drop. It is unlikely that interest rates are rising in a bear market because the Fed tends to be more accommodative during these times and usually lowers rates. So, during bear markets, bonds can be a safe haven, and long bonds may very well increase in price if the Fed lowers the Fed Funds rate. 2022 was an exception to the generalization above. It was a year of rising interest rates and a bear market caused by the large and rapid increases in rates. The lesson here is that not all bear markets are opportunities to own bonds, but most bear markets are not coincident with rates climbing.

2) When the Fed is signaling that rates are coming down or when rates have been increasing and are now flat, with the expectation that they will be coming down soon. As of this

---

[20] Source: https://www.businessinsider.com/'

writing, in December 2023, we have seen many rate hikes starting in early 2022. However, for the last three FOMC meetings, rates have not changed. With inflation coming down, rates are projected to drop twice in 2024. (September and December FOMC meetings) You can look at the long bond ETF, TLT, and use your normal technical analysis techniques to pick an entry point.

Here is a current one-year graph of TLT:

You could have bought TLT around 80 when a 9-bar MA went positive, knowing that they would be easing in 2024. At its present price of $99.04, it has been a good investment. You will note that I prefer bond ETFs to individual issues, partly because it is so tedious to sort through the almost limitless choices of individual bonds. I use TLT for bonds going up and TBF for bonds going down.

3) When inflation is raging. When inflation is rising and expected to continue at least for a year or more, buying TIPS can be a good strategy. (unless interest rates are rising – see the last paragraph in this section). TIPS stands for Treasury Inflation-Protected Securities. Their face value is

adjusted as the Consumer Price Index changes. For example, if you bought a TIPS with a face value of $10,000 and the CPI increases by 3% during the next year, your bond's face value now becomes $10,300. If the coupon rate is 2%, the coupon payments are now calculated on the new face value, and hence increase by 3% in dollar amount from what they were initially. The 2% coupon rate is unchanged, but it is calculated on the larger face value. When inflation has become modest again, you can sell your TIPS and profit from the accumulated gains in face value.

Investors in TIPS should be aware that increases in the face value are taxable in the year they occur as income, even though there is no cash flow to the investor.[21]

One word of caution: Like all bonds, there is interest rate risk. If interest rates increase, the market value of a TIPS goes down. Newly issued TIPS will have a higher coupon rate, and hence, older TIPS will go down in market price to compete.

The following graph shows how the TIPS coupon rate changed over the past 5 years:

---

[21] source: https://www.pimco.com/en-us/resources/education/understanding-treasury-inflation-protected-securities/

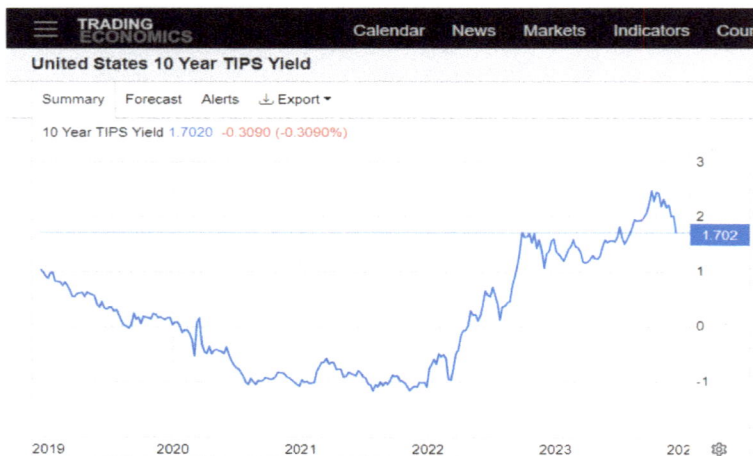

This is where it gets a little complex. As you can see, the coupon rate increased throughout 2022. However, interest rates went up generally and this caused bonds to drop in price. To profit from TIPS, one should have bought them when inflation began in a big way in 2020.

See the following graph of the Consumer Price Index:

There were two possible selling points. The first was in early 2022 when the FED announced that interest rate increases were coming. The second has yet to occur: it requires the TIPS holder to keep the bonds until interest rates drop and sell them at that time. This captures the inflation and avoids the penalty of selling when the coupon yield is not competitive with newly offered TIPS.

Categories > International Data > Countries > United States

☆ **Inflation, consumer prices for the United States** (FPCPITOTLZGUSA)

| Observation: 2022: 8.00280 (+ more) Updated: May 3, 2023 | Units: Percent, Not Seasonally Adjusted | Frequency: Annual | 1Y | 5Y | 10Y | Max 2017-01-01 to 2023-01-01 | DOWNLOAD ⬇ EDIT GRAPH ⚙ |

FRED — Inflation, consumer prices for the United States

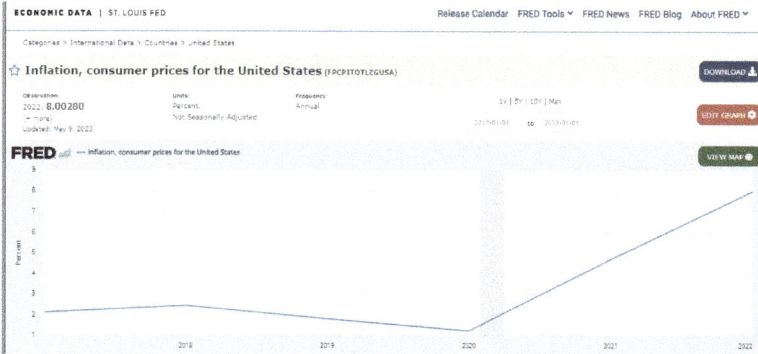

Doing this right is fairly complex, as you can see. For me, there are better and simpler opportunities elsewhere. To keep investing in TIPS simple, one could hold them to maturity. However, if inflation averages 2.5% and the coupon rate is 1.5%, you are realizing a yield of 4%, which is relatively unexciting. Holding them to maturity is very unlikely to outperform stocks.

6.4 Author's Bias

I have known many successful investors and none of them have made more than modest sums in the bond market. Section 6.3 above describes opportune times to invest in bonds or bond ETFs. Since my experience in bond investing is not as deep as it is in equities, automated futures trading, and real estate, it is possible that I have not given sufficient weight to this topic. Hence, feel free to consult other sources on bond investing if you wish. One excellent source is Pimco.com.

Chapter 7: Strategies for Real Estate

Real estate is an important component of the portfolio of individual investors, and there are some important considerations that we will discuss. Some of these you may be familiar with, yet fewer of you have gone through the analysis of how real estate can protect you against inflation during retirement years and how to calculate the amount of inflation hedge you require. The section on inflation in Chapter 8 will go into these considerations. It will be of interest to most readers, even those who own real estate presently. Real estate is not the only way to protect yourself from inflation, but it can be an important part of a plan to protect your future.

We will begin with section 7.1 on Home Ownership, and then discuss the advantages and disadvantages of owning a second property, something that may not happen in the early years, but might be worth serious consideration before retirement. When we use the term Home Ownership, we are speaking of your primary residence, not a second home.

It is certainly true that some real estate investors, especially those who have built a portfolio of properties over the years, have increased their net worth greatly with these investments. Building a large portfolio of properties is not within the scope of this book, and for the average reader of this text, equities are the most significant focus of their investment efforts.

For all of our readers, home ownership is assumed to be a goal. There are strategic considerations for home ownership, and we will discuss them. Less comfortable for many readers is the idea of owning a second property. Our discussion on this subject is important to understand. It's okay to reject the idea of owning a second property, but please read and understand Section 7.2 before you make that decision.

7.1 Home Ownership

This American institution has been a great source of comfort and satisfaction for millions of homeowners and for some, the largest investment they have. Those of us who rented before buying know the joy of being able to make modifications to the home you own without needing permission from a landlord and being certain that property improvements are yours, not someone else's. Over time, most owners make their home fit their needs and tastes, resulting in a home that feels refreshing and relaxing as soon as they enter the front door.

7.1.1. Equity Growth over Time

Here we will look at how equity grows and how to estimate future growth. Let's start by looking at a graph of the Case-Shiller Index from 1987 to November 2023:

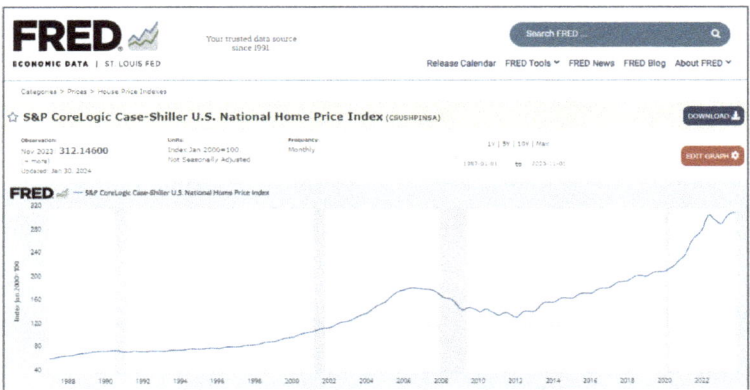

The value in 1987 was 64.13 and the ending value was 312.15. On an annual basis, the increase has been 4.50% per year. Note that, unlike the stock indices, there have been very few significant decreases in the index. The only major drop in home prices was due to the housing crisis of 2007, which we discussed in Chapter

5. Even if you had bought a home at the top of the market in 2006, the drop in prices had completely recovered by 2016 and began a steep climb thereafter. There is good reason to believe that the excesses that preceded the housing crisis will not be repeated. During the years preceding the housing meltdown, mortgages were granted with the lowest set of standards with regard to income, credit history, and, in general, the ability to make the mortgage payments over a long period of time. Fannie Mae and Freddie Mac were buying mortgages from issuers with little regard for the quality of the loans. These excesses were well analyzed after the fact, and standards were adopted to prevent a recurrence of irresponsible lending.

Let's look at a simple hypothetical example of equity growth. We will assume that home prices increase at the rate of 4.5% per year, as they have in the past.

Assume that you buy a home for $300,000 with 15% of that as a down payment. Let's also assume that you have a 30-year mortgage at an interest rate of 5%. Yes, mortgage rates vary a lot, but even if you started with a more expensive rate, you could refinance at or below 5% most of the time. We will assume that homeowner's insurance is $1400/year and that property tax is $2100/year. (You can change any of these parameters if you like).

The graph below is from https://www.mortgagecalculator.org

Mortgage Calculator

Your loan balance will be as follows, just looking at 5-year intervals:

2024	$255,000 ($300,000 less down payment of $45,000)
2029	$229,746
2034	$201,754
2039	$165,830
2044	$119,726
2049	$ 60,558
2054	$ 0.0

Next, we will look at the projected home prices less the original $300,000. to see the increase over time. We will assume a 4.5% annual increase. To do this, we will use the calculator at this URL: https://www.bankrate.com/banking/savings/simple-savings-calculator/

2024	$300,000
2029	$373,855
2034	$465,891
2039	$580,585
2044	$723,514
2049	$901,630
2054	$1,123,595

Putting this into Excel, below is the summary of home value, loan balance, and home equity.

Year	Home Value	Appreciation	Loan Balance	Equity
2024	$300,000	$0	$255,000	$45,000
2029	$373,855	$73,855	$229,746	$144,109
2034	$465,891	$165,891	$201,754	$264,137
2039	$580,585	$280,585	$165,830	$414,755
2044	$723,514	$423,514	$119,726	$603,788
2049	$901,630	$601,630	$60,558	$841,072
2054	$1,123,595	$823,595	$0	$1,123,595

note: Equity is Home Value - Loan Balance

Modeling is important. Does it have weaknesses? Sure. Any assumption can be violated. Nonetheless, models provide us with valuable expectations, allowing us to modify assumptions as needed and add to the model as desired. The data above does not include the amount of the loan payments or rent received, but this is shown in detail in section 7.2.4 for a real-world example.

This model shows how equity grows over time, and unlike other investments, it does not require additions to the portfolio. Yes, maintenance is real and possibly should be deducted from the equity projections. Please do so if you wish. Mortgage interest is deductible, so that is an additional benefit not available to renters. It is not included in the model. Home prices vary widely in the U.S. depending on where you live. You may wish to scale these results to reflect prices in your area or recompute using the BankRate calculator I referenced.

No matter what flaws might be in the assumptions, if you rent for a long period of time instead of owning, you have missed a great opportunity.

Lastly, on the subject of equity, there is great comfort in knowing that if unexpected medical bills come up or if you need cash for any other critical need, a home equity loan is probably available to you after the first few years of ownership.

7.1.2. Tax Advantages

This is a major plus for home ownership. First, the fact that mortgage interest is deductible. This doesn't matter if you take the standard deduction, but if you itemize, it is significant. If you owe $200,000 at some point and the interest rate on your mortgage is 5%, you are paying interest of $10,000 that year. It's part of your mortgage payment, but it's still deductible. If you are paying 15% federal tax, it represents a tax savings of $1500 that year.

Even more importantly, your profit in selling a home is not taxable if it is below the following limits: $250,000 for single filers or $500,000 for married couples. This is huge. With deficits growing in the national budget, tax rates aren't likely to go down, at least in the long run. Because home ownership has been endorsed by the congress for years, this tax advantage remains.

There is no limit on how many times you can use this exemption. If you own a home and it has appreciated close to the limits above after 10 years, you should seriously consider selling it and buying another home. If you refuse to do so, you could end up with a gain of $800,000 and if you are married, paying tax on $300,000 of the appreciation if you sell. Similarly, you could keep a home way too long until you pass away and to your children's surprise, they have a huge tax bill. It could be large enough to force a sale of the home even if they would have preferred to live in it. So, if you have a large gain, think about how nice it would be to own a newer property, or one where you would now prefer to live. The tax mitigating effect of a step-up in basis if you and/or your wife pass away should be understood by homeowners, but the rules depend on whether you are in a community property state, and other factors. This is not within the scope of this book, but is worthy of your time to understand.

7.1.3 When to Start?

The short answer is as early in your life as you can. However, life can throw delaying events at us, such as military service, divorce, or whatever. Start as early as you can. If your first job offers employer matching of part of your 401K deposits, do that first, but get on the home ownership train as soon as you can. If, after 401K deductions, your budget has room for a small mortgage payment, get started. Your first home may come sooner if you are willing to have a roommate. You may wish to buy a home where this can be accommodated. Are interest rates high? You can refinance later. My wife and I bought our first home in 1985 and mortgage rates were 12.5%! Yikes. We were able to refinance before long.

7.1.4 What Size Mortgage?

At the beginning, your first mortgage may be as large as 90% of the market value of the home. What is more complicated is the question of how large a mortgage is appropriate after the home value has greatly increased.

Let's assume that you bought your home years ago and that the value of the home is now three times the amount of the mortgage. Let's also assume that mortgages are now available at an interest rate of 4% per year. If you are in the 20% tax bracket, the interest rate expense of a refi at 4% is 3.2% after tax since the interest is deductible.

Let's also assume that you are confident in investing in equities such that you can realize a gain of 9% per year. This is below the S&P average rate of over 10%. If your home is now worth $450,000 and you have a mortgage balance of $150,000, you could refi and take out $150,000. You now owe $300,000, and you have $150,000 to invest in equities.

If you invest $150,000 and that account increases by 9%, it will appreciate by $13,500

If you paid tax of 20% on this gain, the increase would be .8 x $13,500 = $10,800. At the same time, the interest on your mortgage has gone up by $150,000 x 3.2% = $4,800. The difference, $10,800-$4,800, is $6,000.

The conclusion is that you are $6,000 ahead if you can refi at 4% and gain 9% on your investment in equities. Is this for everyone? No. For some people, this is out of their comfort zone. They should not do it. For others, it is an opportunity and a viable one if they can tolerate the stock market's variations in the short term.

The dream of home ownership often includes the goal of owning your home outright, i.e., no mortgage. What I am suggesting is that this is not necessarily what your ultimate goal should be. It depends on your confidence in yourself, your level of risk tolerance, and what the interest rates are for refinanced mortgages.

7.2 Rental Property

Should you consider owning a second property, one with income from rents? It is not for everyone due to the maintenance requirements and the risk of dealing with bad tenants. Your first inclination may be no, but before you discard the idea altogether, please consider when and why it can be beneficial.

7.2.1 Occasional Compelling Opportunities

There are times when it is compelling to own real estate. The first is when the Fed indicates by quantitative easing that it intends to reflate the economy. First, a couple of quotes from Investopedia:

"Quantitative easing (QE) is a form of monetary policy in which a central bank, like the U.S. Federal Reserve, purchases securities from the open market to reduce interest rates and increase the money supply. Quantitative easing creates new bank reserves, providing banks with more liquidity and encouraging lending and investment. In the United States, the Federal Reserve implements QE policies. Quantitative easing is a form of monetary policy used by central banks to increase the domestic money supply and spur economic activity."

source: https://www.investopedia.com/terms/q/quantitative-easing.asp

We discussed this in Chapter 1, so the quotes are a refresher. In 2009, following the housing crisis that began in 2008, the Fed announced that it would engage in Quantitative Easing. The goal was to increase economic activity and reflate assets. This was a unique opportunity to act upon what the Fed was telling us and to position ourselves for the reflation the Fed predicted.

Housing prices had just gone through a rare downturn, as shown on the chart of the Case-Shiller index in **Section 7.1.1**.

QE started in 2009 and ended in 2014. This was an opportune time to own real estate. During these years, good properties were available from banks that owned them after customer defaults. Your author bought two properties, one in 2011 and one in 2013.

The Case Schiller Index went from 135 to 200 between 2012 and 2018. If you bought a property in 2012 with a 20% down payment, by 2018 the value had increased by 50%, and your down payment had now resulted in equity of not 20%, but much more. Had you purchased a property worth $300,000 with $60,000 down, your equity after 6 years would be $90,000, calculated as $150,000 gain minus $60,000 down.

A second compelling opportunity occurred when the Fed implemented QE in 2020. This was in response to COVID throwing us into recession. This time, it was not only the QE that was the trigger, but also that mortgage rates dropped to around

126

3% for 30-year mortgages. If you can borrow at that rate and buy when the Fed is going to reflate assets, it's compelling. In 2020, the Fed announced that it would purchase $700 billion in assets. Look at the graph above to see how the Case Shiller index responded.

These unique situations don't occur often, but when they do, you must not sit on your hands.

7.2.2 Location Considerations

Section 7.2.1 above talked of when to consider buying a rental property. Here, let's talk about where it should be.

a. Would you live there? If you're considering a single-family home or condo, it's a plus if you look forward to living in it in the future. This is especially true if you are nearing the maximum untaxable gain of $500,000 for married couples or $250,000 for singles on your existing home. You might consider buying the type of home you would like as an upgrade to your current aging home, or in a preferred location. This is not a necessary condition, but a plus. If you buy a property and rent it out, and later decide to move into it, you still have 3 years to sell your original home without losing your tax-free gains. So, your choice of location may be influenced by where you would like to live in the future.

b. Is it a growing area? Case Shiller indices of home prices and other sources can give you information about cities with net in-migration. You might consider buying where solid growth is expected for the next 5 to 10 years. Whether you move into your rental later or not, it is essential to invest where growth trends look solid.

c. Is this a place where you love to vacation? If so, this opens a few possibilities. First, the property might have a living area you can rent, and another you can use. Second, even if it has no quarters for you, some travel to your property may be necessary, and tax-deductible.

d. Are property taxes favorable? Your author has owned property in Hawaii for years, for all of the above reasons. Regarding property tax, it is the lowest of all 50 states.

All of the above are worth taking into account when thinking about where you would invest in income-producing real estate.

7.2.3 Financial Considerations

a. Income and Expenses.

Rent received is income. Repairs and maintenance are tax-deductible. Major items like new appliances are depreciated, and the depreciation is deductible each year. Minor repairs are expensed, i.e., they are subtracted from income during the year they occurred. Examples would be lawn maintenance, replacing smoke detectors, and other similar tasks. Mortgage interest, property taxes, and insurance are deductible each year.

b. Cost Basis if you sell

If you paid $300,000 for the property, that number will be adjusted to be your cost basis when you sell. Expenses incurred during ownership do not alter the cost basis. These are expenses such as minor repairs, insurance, utilities, etc. Capital improvements, like a new roof, increase your cost basis. If you spent $15,000 on a new roof, that is added to your cost basis. Suppose you took depreciation of $12,000 during your ownership, which reduces your cost basis by $12,000. The end result is called your Adjusted Cost Basis.

For more details: https://smartasset.com/taxes/how-to-calculate-cost-basis-on-sale-of-rental-property

c. Taxes if you sell

Assuming that you have not lived in the property, you will pay long-term capital gains taxes on the proceeds of the sale less your adjusted cost basis. The depreciation you took each year during ownership helped you tax-wise. Still, when you sell, you are paying long-term capital gains on the depreciation since it is deducted from your cost basis in calculating the adjusted cost basis.

d. Special consideration if you have lived in the property

If you bought the property, rented it for 8 years, lived in it for 2 years, and then sold after a total of 10 years, the situation becomes a bit more complex. If it became your primary residence after the 8 years it was rented, you may think that when you sell, there will not be any tax on the appreciation. The fact is, if you rented the property for 80% of the time you owned it, as in the example above, you will pay long-term capital gains tax on 80% of the gain in value. This is not commonly understood and can come as an unpleasant surprise to those unaware of it.

7.2.4 A very real example (one of 2)

When considering a rental property as an investment, it is almost impossible to anticipate all of the expenses and costs associated with it. Therefore, I am providing a detailed account of a purchase my wife and I made in 2011, including the rationale behind the purchase, our expenditure during ownership, the gain realized over the 9 years we owned the property, and the taxes incurred in 2020, the year of sale.

a) Rationale for the purchase

As we said in **section 7.2.1,** the housing crisis started in 2008. As the graph of the Case-Shiller index shows, the average home price fell until 2012. The Fed began quantitative easing, also described in **section 7.2.1,** which typically presages asset price increases after enough time for QE to take effect. These two conditions are what we call a "compelling opportunity." Because of the crisis, many properties were in foreclosure or at least bank-owned, meaning that the mortgage was in default and the bank took possession.

In **section 7.2.2**, we spoke of criteria for a good location for a real estate investment. The third of the four criteria was this: Is this a place you love to vacation? We chose the island of Maui in Hawaii. For us, this is our very top choice of places to vacation.

Buying there allowed us to deduct the cost of trips to make improvements, find tenants, etc. Our tax accountant deducted the portion of each trip that was used for the property, and not the portion used for pleasure. We derived great joy from owning a piece of this wonderful island.

The last of the four criteria was this: Are property taxes favorable? Hawaii has the lowest property taxes of all 50 states!

b) How we selected the property that we purchased.

At the time we bought in 2011, there were many bank-owned properties on Maui, and banks generally prefer not to own real estate. In 2011, banks often sold properties for the amount of the outstanding mortgage balance. We decided to buy a single-family residence that was bank-owned, and we were willing to purchase a property that needed work. Many bank-owned properties required work, as the owners, who could no longer afford their mortgage payments, often struggled to afford adequate maintenance as well.

We used a local realtor to help identify candidate properties. We selected a single-family home on the South side of Maui in the town of Kihei. It was (and is) two and a half blocks from the ocean. It had views of the ocean from the exterior decks and the roof over the garage, but not from the interior of the house. The house would be very easy to rent once initial improvements were completed.

c) Pictures of the property

This is a picture from the front. The dumpster was for the old carpeting.

We also needed to replace the old roof shingles since we were replacing the roof.

This picture is of the back of the house.

d) Purchase price, amount as a down payment, and the mortgage terms.

We bought the property for $355,000 from the bank. Yes, this is a very good

price, even for a fixer on Maui. Like many bank-owned properties, it required work, but most of that could be done over a period of years. The first priority was to make it livable and, hence, rentable.

e) Making it rentable

The roof was in terrible condition, so we had it replaced. Some interior painting was required, and the carpet on the middle level and upstairs needed to be replaced. Other improvements could wait, but we wanted to get it rented as soon as possible. Our goal was to have it rented within 3 months from the date of purchase, and we accomplished that. A handyman recommended by the realtor did some of the initial work. After 2 months, he said, "I really like this house. Would you rent it to me?" We did so and allowed him to sublet some space to roommates. He lived there for 8 years and contributed to numerous improvements during that time. Our initial expenditure to make it rentable came to about $30,000, with $15,000 of that being the new roof.

f) Initial cash flow

We provided $70,000 as a down payment, and our mortgage payment was $1846.25 per month. Of course, part of that payment went toward loan reduction, just over $300 per month.

As I mentioned, the handyman rented the house for eight years, with an initial rent of $2200./ per month. Buying a fixer has pluses and minuses, but one plus in this case was that we were above break-even right from the start. We were fortunate to have a handyman as our primary tenant, so we maintained his rate for 5 years before increasing it to $2700 per month.

g) Results from selling the house in 2020.

We sold the house for $788,000. Below is the settlement statement.

Final Seller's Settlement Statement

Item	Debits	Credits
Sales Price		788,000.00
Loan payoff to First Hawaiian Bank ($59,585.62)		
Current Principal	59,069.22	
Accrued Interest	466.40	
Processing Fee	50.00	
Broker's Commission 6%	47,280.00	
To Hawaii Real Estate Team	23,640.00	
To Coldwell Banker Island Prop	23,640.00	
Excise Tax on Commission for Listing Broker	984.84	
Excise Tax on Commission for Selling Broker	984.84	
Paid Outside Closing		
Real Estate Taxes to County of Maui, Real Property Tax Division ((2) 3-9-028-044)		
2nd Half 2019-2020 to County of Maui, Real Property Tax Division $1,917.16 (Seller)		
Pest/Termite Inspection to Bowman Termite & Pest Management	312.50	
HARPTA-Withholding to Hawaii Department of Taxation	57,130.00	
Signing/Notary Services to SnapDocs	150.00	
Deed Preparation to Pro-Docs Hawaii	171.87	
Prorata R.E. Taxes, 04/21/20 to 07/01/20, 70 days @ $10.6509		745.56
Escrow Fees to Old Republic Title & Escrow of Hawaii, Ltd.	856.77	
Additional Charges	187.50	
Mailing/Handling Fee to Old Republic Title & Escrow of Hawaii, Ltd.	31.25	
Wire Service Fee to Old Republic Title & Escrow of Hawaii, Ltd.	52.08	
HARPTA Processing fee to Old Republic Title & Escrow of Hawaii, Ltd.	104.17	
Title Charges		
CLTA Homeowner's to Old Republic Title & Escrow of Hawaii, Ltd.	1,165.50	
Recording Fees	41.00	
Release to the Bureau of Conveyances	41.00	
Conveyance Tax to State of Hawaii	1,576.00	
Due To Seller	618,319.12	
Total	788,745.56	788,745.56

Hawaii withheld more tax than necessary, and we received a $35,000 refund from Hawaii. Here is a summary prepared by our tax accountant on the taxes we paid on the sale of the property:

I did a pro forma tax return to estimate the tax impact of selling the Lanakila property. Income and deductions were consistent with 2019.

Following were the key inputs:

Sale price	788,000
Cost basis	450,000
Sale expenses	54,000
sub-total	284,000
Deprec recapture	115,000
Fed txbl gain on sale	399,000
Fed CG taxes	59,850
Fed NII tax	8,000
Total Federal taxes	67,850
Recommended Pmt to IRS	68,000
Recommended Pmt to CO	5,000
Est refund from HI	35,000

Federal taxes totaled $67,850
Hawaii taxes (after refund) totaled $22,130.
                                         Total Taxes: $89,980.00
The Settlement Statement said Due to Seller: $618,319.
Subtracting taxes, the result is $618,319 - $89,980 =
$528,339.00. This represents the after-tax proceeds. To calculate our net gain, we must subtract the down payment and the costs incurred to improve the property.
The improvements we made over the 9 years of ownership totaled $132,000.
The down payment was $70,000.   70,000.
The amount to be subtracted from the after-tax proceeds:
$202,000.

Our net gain was $528,339 minus $202,000 = $326,339.

Would this have suited you? That is for you to decide. We did quite a bit of touch labor, but we hired out most of the work and acted as a general contractor of sorts. We had a roofer, painter, and carpet supplier arranged to start work the same week we closed escrow. We stayed on Maui for about two weeks after the purchase was complete. Our tenant and handyman did or coordinated the work after we left. For us, this project was really fun. Just being on Maui was terrific. In addition, we were able to deduct travel expenses to Maui since our presence was required for planning the improvements, performing some of the work, and occasionally finding new tenants.

Your circumstances may not permit you to spend as much time on a project as we did. Nonetheless, properties can be bought that are nearly ready to rent and that don't require as much work as this one did.

The bottom line was a gain of $326,000, a great experience, meeting wonderful people, and travelling to Maui. Real estate can be fun and an adventure, too.

7.2.5 Another very real example (The second of 2)

This example is important because it illustrates how significant a real estate investment can be for you personally and financially.

By 2013, housing prices were beginning to recover, but the increases since the housing crisis were still modest. See the Case Shiller graph again in section 7.2.1. On Maui, there were still many bank-owned properties. Interest rates were favorable with 30-year mortgages close to 4%. The Fed was aiding the economy with Fed Funds rates below .25%

We decided to look at MLS listings to see if we could find a second property on Maui. Maui was our choice for the same reasons we cited in the first example (section 7.2.2). The property in example 1 was rented and had no room for us. This time, we were looking for a property with multiple living areas, allowing us to stay in one living area during our visits to Maui while renting out the others. Until then, renting had been quite expensive during our visits.

We found a newer home, built in 2005 by a builder for his own use. The housing crisis decimated his business, and he lost his home in 2013 when the bank took over. It was a two-story home with a mother-in-law suite downstairs, a 500 sq. ft. one-bedroom apartment with its own entrance. Additionally, it had a 500-square-foot cottage on the back of the property with its own fenced yard. We were very excited; We could keep the mother-in-law suite for us and rent out the cottage and main house upstairs. The upstairs has 3 bedrooms, 2 baths, and an office. This property met all of the criteria we mentioned in section 7.2.2.

a. Buying the Property

   We bought the property for $670,000 with a mortgage at 4% (later refinanced at 3.125%). The initial down payment was $200,000. It was unlike the home in example one in that it was rentable right from the start. It was a much newer home (built in 2005) and needed very little work.

b. Pictures of the Property

   These are pictures of the main house and the cottage behind it:

c. Cash Flow from Purchase to 2024.

The table below shows the cash flow if the property is rented without the owners occupying any of the three livable areas. It also shows how the value of the property has increased. The Net column is rent minus mortgage, maintenance, and utilities.

Year	Rent	Mortgage	Maint.	Net	Property
	Market Rate			Per Month	Value
2014	4650	3190	450	1010	720,000
2015	5000	2836	460	1704	750,000
2016	5100	2897	480	1723	790,000
2017	5350	2897	500	1953	850,000
2018	5450	2916	500	2034	910,000
2019	6700	2943	510	3247	1,120,000
2020	7000	2931	535	3534	1,300,000
2021	8350	2948	535	4867	1,430,000
2022	9400	2458	550	6392	1,570,000
2023	9900	2233	555	7112	1,540,000
2024	9900	2233	570	7097	1,610,000

You will note that the mortgage payment dropped in 2022. It was refinanced at a lower interest rate. We occupied part of the property starting in 2022, so the rents we received were the same through 2021, but lower for

2022 and 2023. Occupying part of the property has been a massive benefit for us.

d. Status as of June 2024

We still own this property. We have made remodels and improvements along the way, amounting to approximately $130,000. The house, being much newer than that of example #1, did not require drastic changes, just upgrades. This example shows what can happen when a real estate investment is well chosen and well timed. The value today, according to Zillow, is $ 1.6 million. We have a place to stay on Maui, and we are thrilled to be here almost six months a year. By now, we are able to rent the mother-in-law suite and cottage, and keep the upstairs for us and our visitors from the mainland.

The message here is that there are times when real estate is a compelling opportunity. As we said in the opening paragraphs of this chapter, "It's ok to reject the idea of owning a second property, but please read and understand Section 7.2 before you make that decision."

Section III
Putting It All Together

Chapter 8: Top-Level Planning

8.1 Assess your strengths

We all have different psychological makeup, and here we encourage you to take inventory.

a. Preferred Level of Focus

Are you a conceptual thinker, preferring not to let details interfere with higher-level considerations, or are you a detail-oriented person who tends toward analysis? There is a lot of room for both types and blends of the two, but it is helpful to realize where you fit on this scale. Philosophers are good examples of conceptual thinkers. It is not hard to imagine a philosopher who is unaware that his clothes don't match and are seriously wrinkled. An example of a detail-oriented individual might be an accountant at a large company who is unconcerned about the company's product offerings and not interested in what they are planning for the future. He is more focused on the company's balance sheet and how his own 401K is doing. Conceptual thinkers excel at analyzing macroeconomic trends and can provide valuable insights to an investment advisor managing his funds. He may not be interested in security analysis or market timing. Detail-oriented people are often skilled at stock picking, timing their buys and sells wisely, and following detailed processes.

b. Risk Tolerance

How tolerant or averse are you to risk? We all know that investing involves some losses, and the question here is whether you can tolerate them with ease, or whether they will throw you into a difficult place psychologically until your portfolio is in a happier state. This is loosely related to

a)   above, but involves other factors. Past misfortunes can result in low tolerance for uncertainty and for occasional losses. One's present financial situation also has an impact here. With a large pool of assets, you may not be worried about market fluctuation. That is very different from the feelings that a person may have if he has very little in savings. You should make an informal self-assessment on this subject.

If you are highly risk-averse, buying and selling stocks yourself may not be optimal for you. These decisions are best made using data and analysis. The risk-averse person has a more difficult time keeping emotion out of the process.

c.   Position on a Team

Do you prefer to manage people, teams, and organizations, or do you prefer a well-defined set of responsibilities for which you are personally accountable? This is somewhat related to a) and b) above, but a person's preferences here depend on other factors as well. If your career experiences have shown that you are good at leading people, you may gravitate toward being a team leader. If you believe that your success can't be managed if it depends greatly on others, then you may prefer having a well-defined set of responsibilities that you can execute with minimal dependence on others. Leader types excel when working with investment advisors and others who manage their funds. People who prefer their own well-defined set of responsibilities often do well at stock selection, timing their buys and sells, and keeping their eyes closely on their investments.

8.2 Financial Planning

Some people specialize in financial planning. This is how Investopedia defines the role of such a professional:

"A financial planner is a professional who helps individuals and organizations create a strategy to meet their long-term financial goals. Typically, a financial planner will help map out a plan for budgeting, saving, investing, and retirement planning. Although many financial planners assist individual clients through their own practice, they might also work for a bank, wealth management firm, or a non-profit organization."

Let's defer for a moment the question of whether you should use a financial planner. First, more on what they can do for you. A financial planner will recommend whether you need a tax-sheltered account for your children's future tuition. He will recommend how much life insurance you should have. He will advise you on the use of IRAs, whether Roth or traditional, and the use of 401K plans. He will suggest how much of your income should be allocated to investments and how much should be kept in savings. He will advise you regarding potential investments in real estate. He will advise you on when to start Social Security and how you should be positioned when you retire. Many people have not given serious thought or effort to financial planning, and for some of them, it has not gone well. You probably have a friend or relative whose earnings were adequate over the years, but despite that, they do not have adequate assets for a comfortable retirement. I personally have more than a few friends or acquaintances who fit that description. One couple I have known for over 40 years has never owned a piece of real estate and still rents today. They are largely on social security and have only modest savings. During their working years, they drove fancy cars, travelled often, and earned at least twice the average family income in the U.S. They now rely a great deal on their children. A competent financial planner would never let a client end up like this. You can ponder similar stories from your own experience.

Regarding the previously deferred question on whether you should use a financial planner, I believe that almost all of us should use the services of a financial planner occasionally. Their services are fee-based and affordable. The rules change often on social security, 401(k)s, IRAs, and inherited assets. A professional financial planner should have the knowledge and experience to guide you to a successful roadmap for your journey. See your financial planner after your initial meetings every five years or so, and following any significant changes in your circumstances.

MISTAKES OR LAPSES IN PLANNING CAN COST YOU DEARLY; GOOD PLANNING PAYS HUGE DIVIDENDS.

8.3 Tax Planning

This is a definition of tax planning according to Investopedia.com:

"Tax planning is the analysis of a financial situation or plan to ensure that all elements work together to allow you to pay the lowest taxes possible. A plan that minimizes how much you pay in taxes is referred to as tax-efficient. Tax planning should be an essential part of an individual investor's financial plan. Reduction of tax liability and maximizing the ability to contribute to retirement plans are crucial for success."

Here are some of the factors to consider in tax planning:

a. Contributing to 401K plans and/or IRAs, whether traditional or Roth. Taking full advantage of employer matching is important. Contributions to a 401K plan are usually deductible, i.e., not taxed, whereas Roth IRA contributions are made with after-tax dollars.

b. Holding investments for over a year, so that any sale is treated as long-term capital gains. For most of us, the tax on these gains is 15%. Short-term capital gains are taxed as ordinary income.

c. Avoiding the sale of appreciated assets in high-income years. If you had windfall income in a particular year, you might consider avoiding the sale of appreciated assets. Don't put yourself in a higher tax bracket unnecessarily.

d. Selling assets with losses to offset gains. In a year when you had significant short-term gains, you may wish to sell any investments with losses to mitigate the tax liability.

e. Real estate. If you need extra help with keeping your taxes down, rental properties can be a big help. Both deductible expenses and depreciation can be significant.

f. Charitable donations. These are deductible (with limits) and should be phased so they are taken in the highest income years.

g. Enterprise Zone donations. Some states permit donations to qualifying charities in Enterprise Zones to give partial credit towards state taxes.

h. Mitigation of taxes on inherited assets.

Is your Financial Planner the go-to person to do tax planning? No. While he is an expert in all of the things we mentioned in paragraph 8.2, he likely knows less about current tax law than a dedicated tax attorney or advisor. Most of our readers have someone else prepare their tax returns. Selecting the right person for that job requires careful consideration. They should be qualified to help you with tax planning, not just the preparation of your returns. TurboTax and other software platforms will not do that for you. Selecting the right person for tax planning and preparation should be given attention similar to selecting a financial planner or an MD.

A FINANCIAL PLANNER AND A TAX EXPERT ARE TWO OF THE MOST IMPORTANT PEOPLE ON YOUR TEAM.

8.4 Investment Management

You have a number of alternatives from which to select expertise to supplement your own. Let's assume you plan to allocate a percentage of your funds to individual stocks for investment, selecting the timing. Let's call this active investing. For the remainder of your funds, you would like the help of a professional. Let's look at the most likely alternatives. Many people put all of these under the title of passive investing.

a. Index Funds.

The ETF SPY is like investing in the S&P 500 Index. QQQ is like investing in the Nasdaq index. There are others, like Dow Jones funds and Small Caps. Whereas 80% of mutual funds do not have returns as great as the S&P index, SPY surely will. If you invest in SPY, just be sure you don't suffer the intense pain of bear markets. You can protect yourself using the methods discussed in **Chapter 5**, Strategies for Equities. The management fees are very modest for index funds. There are even inverse funds. SDS, for example, mimics the daily performance of being short the S&P index and is leveraged at 2x. That is, a $1,000 long position in SDS is like being short $2,000 of SPY. Yes, index funds can be part of the portfolio you manage, but they are also called "passive investments" because many investors use them for long-term wealth accumulation without active management. After reading the earlier chapters of this book, you know that I do not consider index funds something to ignore in bear markets. In fact, keeping your losses modest in bear markets while using SPY and/or other index-based ETFs is one of the easiest ways to beat the performance of the S&P index.

b. Mutual Funds. There are many of them, but as we mentioned above, 80% will not perform as well as the S&P index. Management fees must be considered. Morningstar.com is a wonderful source of data on mutual funds. Most mutual funds in general have done poorly in bear markets, and you must manage your risk using the methods of Chapter 5, even if you buy mutual funds.

Note: Berkshire Hathaway (BRK.B) is actively managed and can be used by investors just as a mutual fund. It outperforms most mutual funds and has lower management fees.

c. Bond Funds. We described TLT, a long-duration bond ETF, and TBF, an inverse bond ETF, in **Chapter 6**, Strategies for Bonds. We often are given great insight into the direction of interest rates by the Fed in their communications (see Chapter 1). Buying a bond ETF is much easier than buying individual bond issues, and can be particularly safe and profitable in bear markets. The fund managers of these ETFs handle the buying and selling of bonds in their portfolio, but you remain in charge of determining when to be long or short the bond market and when to avoid involvement with bonds.

d. Investment Advisors. They typically charge fees between .75% and 1.2% per year on the funds they are managing. It is more difficult to assess past performance than it is for a mutual fund or an index fund. Morningstar won't help you evaluate a financial advisor. You can look at charts of past performance on Barchart.com for many mutual funds, and for all of the index funds, but investment advisors tailor each account to the client, and their past performance is difficult to assess. You may end up selecting one with a reputable firm, and, after discussing your priorities, letting them manage some of your portfolio to see how it goes. An investment advisor from a firm with a strong research arm is preferable. Morgan Stanley and Charles Schwab are two. I would ensure that any investment advisor managing your funds respects your wishes regarding risk management, particularly in bear markets, and when to favor growth stocks over value. Your skills in this area, following the guidance in chapter 5, are likely superior to his. Choosing an investment advisor from a large organization assures you that he or she has the proper certifications.

Each of the choices above requires your involvement to achieve good outcomes. You may have thought that using an investment advisor relieves you of any decision-making, but it isn't that simple. If 80% of mutual funds perform worse than the S&P 500 index, is it reasonable to expect your investment advisor to do better than the S&P index? That may not be a realistic expectation, and you must factor in the fees an investment advisor charges. There is another reason that you may not wish just to hand the reins to a financial advisor: You bought and read this book. Why read any books about investing if you are going to delegate all of it to someone else? Using an investment advisor can be helpful to manage part of your portfolio. If, however, the market is in bear territory and the weekly charts confirm the downtrend, you must have a conversation with your IA and direct him to move a significant part of your holdings into cash, a short-term bond fund, or a bond ETF such as TLT or TBF. If we are in a bull market and the seasonal influences are positive, you probably should be more in growth stocks than defensive stocks. If your IA hasn't positioned your account accordingly, it's time for a chat (while remembering that you are the boss)

One way to look at what we have said in this chapter is to make an analogy with an orchestra. Stock selection, Index ETFs, Mutual Funds, Market Timing, and Investment Advisors are instruments. You are the orchestra leader, and only you can create music with these instruments. Much of this book, especially the chapters on strategies, is focused on giving you the ability to make music. You will be able to do so, but just as the orchestra leader doesn't delegate to the violinists the responsibility for the total performance, you cannot delegate the end results over time to any particular brokerage, advisor, or fund manager. We put items a) thru d) above in the category of passive investments. The term passive is not to be an opiate for your lack of involvement. With your active participation, you can achieve above-average results.

8.5 Products from the Thought Processes of this chapter, Chapter 8

a. The amount available for you to invest. (from the Financial Plan)

b. Your assessment of your risk tolerance

c. Your preferences on higher or lower levels of thought

d. Your preferences, leader or individual contributor?

e. The percent of your funds you will personally manage. (from a, b, and c, and d above)

f. The passive investments will you use (from the list in section 8.4)

g. Guidance about long term and short-term investments.(from your Tax Planner)

These products are inputs to the creation of an execution plan, the subject of Chapter 9.

Chapter 9: Execution Plan

In this chapter, we discuss the periodic tasks that should be performed on both monthly and weekly intervals. It will be tailored to your circumstances and personality. This chapter is a companion to Chapter 8 and will make use of many of the thought processes there, and especially four of the products of Chapter 8 listed in Section 8.5. The products are the following: (a,e,f, and g in section 8.5)

1. The amount available for you to invest
2. The percentage of your funds you will personally manage.
3. The passive investments you will use (from the list in section 8.4)
4. Guidance about long-term and short-term investments (from your Tax Planner)

Developing these products required serious thought and introspection on your part, and I congratulate you on doing the critical thinking that this reflects. These products will not only help create an execution plan, but they will enable future conversations with your financial planner, tax planner, and investment advisor (if you use one) to be well-structured and fruitful.

LET'S DEFINE THE PERIODIC TASKS YOU SHOULD PERFORM

1. **Monthly Tasks**

   It is crucial to assess the factors influencing the direction of the broad markets both now and over the next few months. To do that, there are 3 recommended tasks:

a. Assess the level and direction of interest rates.

Below is a graph of the Fed Funds rate taken from Chapter 1 on the Federal Reserve System. You will recall how the Federal Open Market Committee often drops the Fed Funds Rate dramatically during recessions. You can also see that these drops are usually followed by strong periods for stocks.

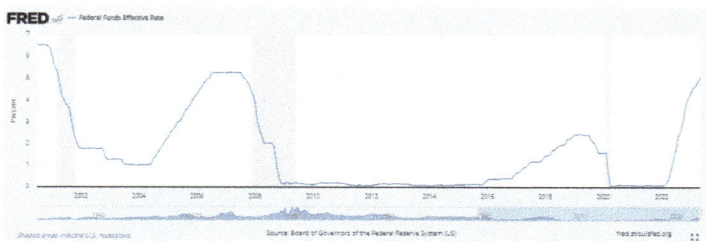

Listen to the Fed chairman's remarks after each FOMC meeting and his assessment of the direction of rates going forward.

b. Look at the weekly charts of the S&P index.

In section 5.2 of the chapter on Strategies for Equities, we used 12-bar and 30-bar moving averages on a weekly chart of the S&P 500 index. Section 5.2 is entitled,

"Allocation to Stocks – What % Should You Be Invested?" Take another look at section 5.2. Whether the 12-bar MA is above or below the 30-bar MA is an excellent indicator of market direction. In section 5.2, we recommended being at least 80% long when the 12-bar moving average is above the 30-bar. Take a look at how these two moving averages would have kept you out of the market in 2022, a down year.

c. Look at Investor Business Daily's recommendation on what percent to invest in stocks. Their recommendation has its weaknesses, but is valuable nonetheless. These recommendations are worth tracking and can be particularly helpful in giving you caution even when the 12 bar MA is above the 30 on the weekly chart of the S&P.

They can help you reduce your exposure to equities even before the 12-bar MA falls below the 30-bar.

Current Outlook:
Market Exposure Level: 40%-60%

Stock Market Exposure

| 0-20% | 20-40% | 40-60% | 60-80% | 80-100% |

40% to 60% Invested

d. Consider the seasonal factors. Recall this table from Chapter 5:

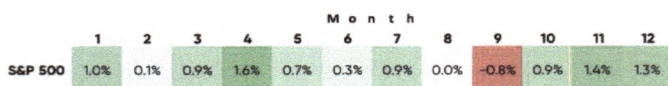

	Month											
	1	2	3	4	5	6	7	8	9	10	11	12
S&P 500	1.0%	0.1%	0.9%	1.6%	0.7%	0.3%	0.9%	0.0%	-0.8%	0.9%	1.4%	1.3%

Once you have looked at these four items, you should have as good an assessment of the market's near-term direction as anyone, and you should have a very good basis for deciding how much you should invest for the next month. You should decide what percentage to hold long over the next month, as this is a monthly task. Start with the IBD recommendation and make adjustments to account for seasonal factors and economic projections from the Fed and major banks. This is part art and part science, but you will be far ahead of the pack in making these assessments and adjusting your exposure accordingly.

2. Weekly Tasks.

From the methods in Chapter 8, you have decided whether you will use passive investments, individual stocks, or a combination of both. The weekly tasks are simpler if you use only passive investments because you are not evaluating individual stocks. Therefore, you are not conducting fundamental and technical analyses of companies, nor are you selecting exit strategies for those that are underperforming. Additionally, you are not maintaining a Watch List of stocks that you do not own but which have merit and which you may consider buying in the future. For investors who use passive investments only, I would recommend one weekly task: Read Investors Business Daily. It will help broaden your perspectives on investing, and you will likely enjoy reading it.

A. Weekly Tasks for investors who use only passive investments

As we said in chapter 8, we are including in the term passive investments index funds (ETFs), mutual funds, bond ETFs, and funds managed for you by an investment manager. Index funds like SPY (S&P 500) and QQQ (Nasdaq 100) use a large basket of stocks to mirror the indices, and any adjustments to them are made by the managers of the ETF. Mutual funds and funds managed for you by an investment manager include active management, which is reflected in higher management fees than index ETFs. That said, professional management is what you are paying for, and it does relieve you of the work involved in stock selection, risk management, and timing of entries and exits.

The only weekly task I recommend for investors who do not buy individual stocks is this: Read Investor's Business

Daily. It will broaden your perspectives, and you will probably find it relevant and interesting.

B. Weekly Tasks for owners of individual stocks

    i.   Keep and update a spreadsheet of the stocks you own and those on your watch list. Include the dollar amount value for each stock and any stop orders. By stop orders, I mean orders to exit the position if it falls below a certain price. If you enter a stop market order for a stock, add it to your spreadsheet. Below your list of stocks (one per row), leave a few blank rows, and then list stocks on your watchlist. Use one or two columns for comments for the stocks you own and also for stocks on your watchlist.

        Here's an example for an investor with 3 accounts:

	A	B	C	D	E	F	G	H	I
			Account: Schw 041	Account: IRA	Account: Inh IRA	Total $ by Stock	Stop Order?	Comments	Date of Comment
1	Stock	Industry							
2									
3	ONON	Ret		22,500		22,500		Consider Sell	2/10/2025
4	ANET	Tech	35,100		23,200	58,300	Yes		
5	AVGO	Tech	43,700	12,900		56,600			
6	COST	Retail			34,700	34,700			
7	DUOL	SW				0			
8	GEV	Energ	25,900	15,200		41,100	Yes		
9	JPM	Bank	34,200		18,700	52,900	Yes		
10	MRX	Fin	14,800	14,800		29,600	Yes		
11	MSFT	Tech		19,300	19,300	38,600			
12	VRSN	Dig Infr	x			0			
13	VRT	Dig Infr			x	0			
14	WMT	Retail	34,600		34,600	69,200	Yes		
15						403,500		Total Invested	
16	CASH %		26	35	25%	29%		%Cash	
17									
18	Watch List:								
19	EAT								
20	SBUX								
21	AXP								
22	ASTS								

Add any stocks to your watchlist that you may wish to buy in the future. Good sources are the IBD top 50 list, stocks owned by Berkshire Hathaway, and stocks recommended by an advisory service like Motley Fool or Seeking Alpha. Also, drop from your watchlist any stocks that no longer seem worth tracking.

ii.   Evaluate any stock you are considering adding to your portfolio. Use the methods of Chapter 3, Charts and Technical Analysis, and the methods of Chapter 4, Fundamental Analysis of Equities. If you are a subscriber to Investor Business Daily, you can look at their evaluation of the stock. Log in at investors.com and enter the stock symbol in the search bar. You will see a detailed assessment there. I do not buy stocks if the IBD evaluation is below 85. Also, look at recent news articles on the company. Put the symbol in the search bar of Barchart.com and scroll down the left-hand column. Under COMPANY, you will see News and Headlines. Before buying a stock, read any recent posts listed there. On timing, only buy a stock if the 9-bar moving average on the daily chart is going up.

iii.   Decisions on Buy Orders and Stop Orders

I tend to do my weekly tasks on the weekend. I prefer this approach because the markets are closed, and I am not distracted by real-time changes. After reviewing the charts of your stocks, determine if you need to enter or adjust any existing stop orders. You can do that when the market is closed or when it is open. If you have decided to buy a stock, decide on how many shares and look at the chart again on the day you enter your buy order. I prefer to enter any market orders to buy only after 11 am New York time. The first hour and a half are volatile, and I want to make sure I am not buying into a downtrend.

Appendix A:
Essential Resources

The following resources are essential enough for you to be familiar with each one. They are mentioned in the text and summarized for you here.

1. Investors Business Daily.
   - This weekly newspaper is a must-read. Subscribe to it and read the first section each week.
   - New articles are updated daily on their website, investors.com. If you want to find out what has just moved the markets, and what upcoming events will, this is where to start.
   - As a subscriber, you have access to stock evaluations. Just type the ticker symbol in the search bar. Here is an example:

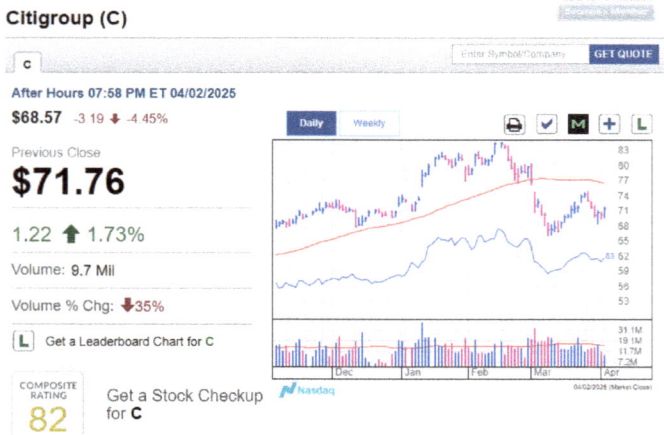

2. Barchart.com

- Their charts are excellent and free of charge. Just click on Snapshot Chart on the left side after entering a ticker symbol in the search bar.
- Before you look at the charts, if you want to see summary statistics on any stock,
  select Price Overview from the top of the list on the left. This is an example of what you will see:

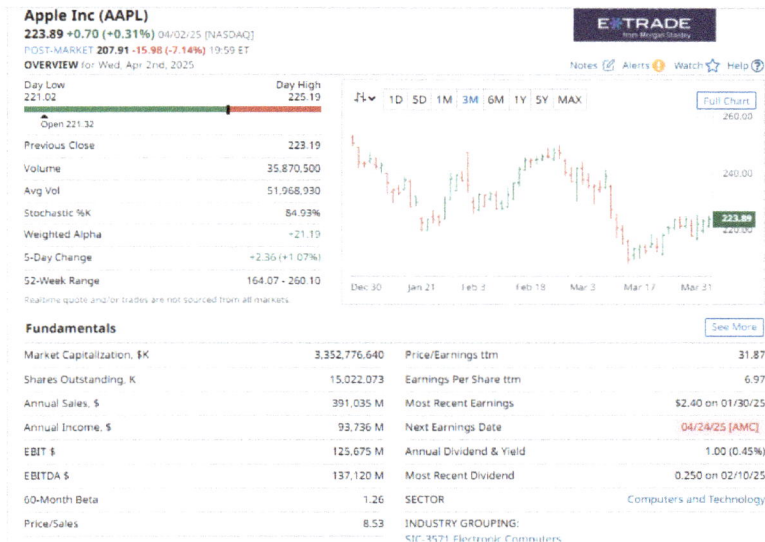

3. StockAnalysis.com

- This website provides a list of top stocks as recommended by financial advisors. To access the full list, you must be a subscriber, but that costs just $10/month. Here is an example which is displayed when you select Top Stocks from the list on the left side:

Top 50 Strong Buy Stocks

The top 50 "Strong Buy" stocks according to the best performing Wall Street analysts.

Strong Buy stocks according to stock analysts with a star rating of 4 or higher. These analysts have much higher accuracy and returns than average. Stocks are sorted by upside potential. Only stocks rated by 10 or more top-performing analysts are included.

Top Stocks

No.	Symbol	Company Name	Top Rating	Top Analysts	Top PT	Top PT Upside (%)	Market Cap
1	TTD	The Trade Desk, Inc.	Strong Buy	12	125.50	122.91%	27.93B
2	MRVL	Marvell Technology, Inc.	Strong Buy	21	120.67	90.84%	54.76B
3	MDB	MongoDB, Inc.	Strong Buy	10	328.00	87.03%	14.63B
4	VRT	Vertiv Holdings Co	Strong Buy	10	140.20	81.32%	29.36B
5	MKSI	MKS Instruments, Inc.	Strong Buy	9	141.78	74.43%	5.48B

- Explore the website; there are many features, including all the latest news on the stock you selected

4. StockCharts.com

- This service provides many of the same chart styles as Barchart.com, but it offers one very useful feature not common among charting services. It allows you to display two symbols on one chart. If you want to look at how two indices correlate, for example, you can plot them both together. You first make a chart for one symbol. Then, under Indicator, select Price, and enter the second indicator in the Parameter box.

5. FOMC Calendar

- You should listen to the interest rate announcement and the statement by the Chairman of the Federal Reserve System. The financial channels on TV broadcast this information at 2 pm Eastern Time on the second day of the two-day meetings. Here's a link to the FOMC Calendar: https://www.federalreserve.gov/monetarypolicy/fomccalendars.html

You will hear the Fed's projections for the economy and interest rates.

6. Investopedia

- Investopedia.com is a bit like an encyclopedia for investors. You will find definitions of terms and articles explaining terms and concepts. Below is a pic of the screen from Investopedia.com after entering Minimum Required Distribution in the search bar:

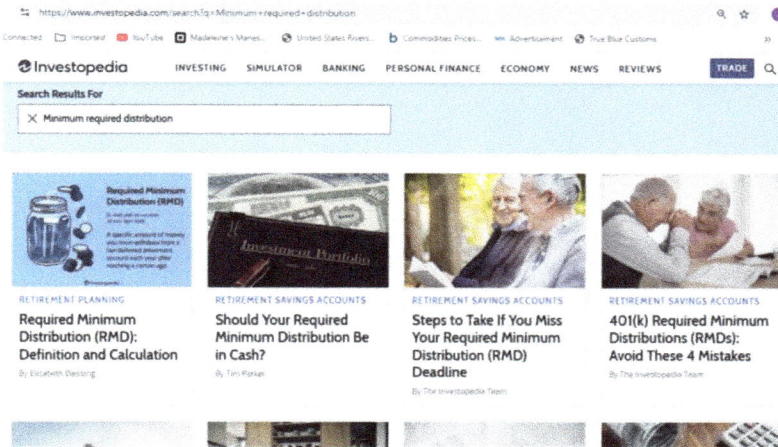

- There are articles about almost anything you can think of relating to investing.

7. Afterwork

- This book, by 2 financial advisors, contains great wisdom about that how to live a post-work life that has meaning, fulfillment and joy. It debunks the popular thought that financial success brings all of these things. It does not.

- Many of the readers of Strategic Investing will be financially successful, but feeling fulfilled and of value will result from other sources including generosity, faith, stimulating activities, learning new things.

- I, your author, have given away over 20 copies of Afterwork to friends and associates. It is worth your attention. Life is not just about wealth, and Afterwork captures the essence of success in retirement in the broadest sense.

The authors of Afterwork are Joel Malick and Alex Lippert.

Appendix B:
Quotes by Warren Buffett

The following quotes by Warren Buffett are provided courtesy of investingansers.com

A few may differ in some respects from what this book recommends. Nonetheless, it is always worthwhile to listen to the masters.

https://investinganswers.com/articles/50-warren-buffett-quotes-inspire-your-investing

Many people follow Warren Buffett as a source of wisdom, not just as a master investor. In an article on April 17, 2025, there is a description of how Melinda Gates relies on wise mentors: Despite having over $14 billion to her name, Melinda French Gates, too, gets anxious and worried about the impact of her work.

"But, just like the many Americans who look up to her (Melinda Gates) for inspiration, she leans on others when times are tough. In fact, French Gates has revealed she likes to write down quotes and wise advice from her hugely successful friends so that she can "replay" it again later in her head—one of those voices being none other than fellow billionaire Warren Buffett.

source: https://www.yahoo.com/finance/news/melinda-french-gates-shares-advice-160551387.html

1. 'Rule No. 1: Never lose money. Rule No. 2: Never forget Rule No. 1.'

2. 'A very rich person should leave his kids enough to do anything, but not enough to do nothing.'

3. 'It's class warfare; my class is winning, but they shouldn't be.'

4. 'If you're in the luckiest 1% of humanity, you owe it to the rest of humanity to think about the other 99%.'

5. 'It takes 20 years to build a reputation and five minutes to ruin it. If you think about that, you'll do things differently.'

6. 'Of the billionaires I have known, money just brings out the basic traits in them. If they were jerks before they had money, they are simply jerks with a billion dollars.'

7. 'The business schools reward difficult, complex behavior more than simple behavior, but simple behavior is more effective.'

8. 'You do things when the opportunities come along. I've had periods in my life when I've had a bundle of ideas come along, and I've had long dry spells. If I get an idea next week, I'll do something. If not, I won't do a damn thing.'

9. 'Can you really explain to a fish what it's like to walk on land? One day on land is worth a thousand years of talking about it, and one day running a business has exactly the same kind of value.'

10. 'You only have to do a very few things right in your life so long as you don't do too many things wrong.'

11. 'It's far better to buy a wonderful company at a fair price than a fair company at a wonderful price.'

12. 'Only buy something that you'd be perfectly happy to hold if the market shut down for 10 years.'

13. 'We simply attempt to be fearful when others are greedy and to be greedy only when others are fearful.'

14. 'Risk is a part of God's game, alike for men and nations.'

15. 'Should you find yourself in a chronically leaking boat, energy devoted to changing vessels is likely to be more productive than energy devoted to patching leaks.'

16. 'We believe that according to the name 'investors', to institutions that trade actively is like calling someone who repeatedly engages in one-night stands a 'romantic.''

17. 'Chains of habit are too light to be felt until they are too heavy to be broken.'

18. 'It's better to hang out with people better than you. Pick out associates whose behavior is better than yours and you'll drift in that direction.'

19. 'Let blockheads read what blockheads wrote.'

20. 'Our favorite holding period is forever.'

21. 'I don't look to jump over seven-foot bars; I look around for one-foot bars that I can step over.'

22. 'If a business does well, the stock eventually follows.'

23. 'Why not invest your assets in the companies you really like? As Mae West said, 'Too much of a good thing can be wonderful.''

24. 'Price is what you pay. Value is what you get.'

25. 'Wide diversification is only required when investors do not understand what they are doing.'

26. 'Time is the friend of the wonderful company, the enemy of the mediocre.'

27. 'Only when the tide goes out do you discover who's been swimming naked.'

28. 'In the business world, the rearview mirror is always clearer than the windshield.'

29. 'Risk comes from not knowing what you're doing.'

30. 'Look at market fluctuations as your friend rather than your enemy; profit from folly rather than participate in it.'

31. 'There seems to be some perverse human characteristic that likes to make easy things difficult.'

32. 'If you are in a poker game and after 20 minutes you don't know who the patsy is, then you're the patsy.'

33. 'Wall Street is the only place that people ride to in a Rolls-Royce to get advice from those who take the subway.'

34. 'The rich invest in time, the poor invest in money.'

35. 'Beware of geeks bearing formulas.'

36. 'Without passion, you don't have energy. Without energy, you have nothing.'

37. 'I get to do what I like to do every single day of the year.'

38. 'I never attempt to make money on the stock market. I buy on the assumption they could close the market the next day and not re-open it for five years.'

39. 'If past history was all that is needed to play the game of money, the richest people would be librarians.'

40. 'The investor of today does not profit from yesterday's growth.'

41. 'The smarter the journalists are, the better off the society is to a degree. People read the press to inform themselves, and the better the teacher, the better the student body.'

42. 'We enjoy the process far more than the proceeds.'

43. 'Focus on your customers and lead your people as though their lives depend on your success.'

44. 'I have no idea about timing. It's easier to tell what will happen than when it will happen. I would say that what is going on in terms of trade policy is going to have very important consequences.'

45. 'Cash never makes us happy. It's better to have the money burning a hole in Berkshire's pocket than resting comfortably in someone else's.'

46. 'Never invest in a business you can't understand.'

47. 'Derivatives are financial weapons of mass destruction.'

48. 'We've used derivatives for many, many years. I don't think derivatives are evil, per se; I think they are dangerous. ...So, we use lots of things daily that are dangerous, but we generally pay some attention to how they're used. We tell the cars how fast they can go.'

49. 'Only when you combine sound intellect with emotional discipline do you get rational behavior.'

50. 'I buy expensive suits. They just look cheap on me.'

Appendix C:
Quotes by Peter Lynch

"Peter Lynch (born January 19, 1944)[1] is an American investor, mutual fund manager, author, and philanthropist. As the manager of the Magellan Fund[2] at Fidelity Investments between 1977 and 1990, Lynch averaged a 29.2% annual return [3], consistently more than double the S&P 500 stock market index, and made it the best-performing mutual fund in the world.[4][5] During his 13-year tenure, assets under management increased from US$18 million to $14 billion.[6] A proponent of value investing, Lynch wrote and co-authored a number of books and papers on investing strategies, including One Up on Wall Street, published by Simon & Schuster in 1989." https://en.wikipedia.org/wiki/Peter_Lynch

Below are some of his quotes courtesy of investinganswers.com.

https://investinganswers.com/articles/51-peter-lynch-quotes-empower-your-investing

1. In stocks, as in romance, ease of divorce is not a sound basis for commitment.

2. The key to making money in stocks is not to get scared out of them.

3. There's no shame in losing money on a stock. Everybody does it. What is shameful is to hold On to a stock, or worse, to buy more of it when the fundamentals are deteriorating.

4. Behind every stock is a company. Find out what it's doing.

5. Owning stocks is like having children -- don't get involved with more than you can handle.

6. If you don't study any companies, you have the same success buying stocks as you do in a poker game if you bet without looking at your cards.

7. Average investors can become experts in their own field and can pick winning stocks as effectively as Wall Street professionals by doing just a little research.

8. You have to keep your priorities straight if you plan to do well in stocks.

9. The basic story remains simple and never-ending. Stocks aren't lottery tickets. There's a company attached to every share.

10. People who want to know how stocks fared on any given day ask, 'Where did the Dow close?' I'm more interested in how many stocks went up versus how many went down. These so-called advance/decline numbers paint a more realistic picture.

11. When people discover they are no good at baseball or hockey, they put away their bats and their skates and they take up amateur golf or stamp collecting or gardening. But when people discover they are no good at picking stocks, they are likely to continue to do it anyway.

12. If you hope to have more money tomorrow than you have today, you've got to put a chunk of your assets into stocks. Sooner or later, a portfolio of stocks or stock mutual funds will turn out

to be a lot more valuable than a portfolio of bonds, CDs, or money-market funds.

13. Investing in stocks is an art, not a science, and people who've been trained to rigidly quantify everything have a big disadvantage.

14. All the math you need in the stock market, you get in the fourth grade.

15. If you're prepared to invest in a company, then you ought to be able to explain why in simple language that a fifth grader could understand, and quickly enough so the fifth grader won't get bored.

16. Your investor's edge is not something you get from Wall Street experts. It's something you already have. You can outperform the experts if you use your edge by investing in companies or industries you already understand.

17. If you can't find any companies that you think are attractive, put your money in the bank until you discover some.

18. Time is on your side when you own shares of superior companies.

19. In the long run, a portfolio of well-chosen stocks and/or equity mutual funds will always outperform a portfolio of bonds or a money-market account. In the long run, a portfolio of poorly chosen stocks won't outperform the money left under the mattress.

20. The worst thing you can do is invest in companies you know nothing about. Unfortunately, buying stocks on ignorance is still a popular American pastime.

21. I'm always fully invested. It's a great feeling to be caught with your pants up.

22. Never invest in any idea you can't illustrate with a crayon.

23. My high-tech aversion caused me to make fun of the typical biotech enterprise: $100 million in cash from selling shares, One hundred PhDs, 99 microscopes, and zero revenues.

24. You can find good reasons to scuttle your equities in every morning paper and on every broadcast of the nightly news.

25. Equity mutual funds are the perfect solution for people who want to own stocks without doing their own research.

26. Gentlemen who prefer bonds don't know what they're missing.

27. If you can follow only one bit of data, follow the earnings (assuming the company in question has earnings). I subscribe to the crusty notion that sooner or later earnings make or break an investment in equities. What the stock price does today, tomorrow, or next week is only a distraction.

28. All you need for a lifetime of successful investing is a few big winners, and the pluses from those will overwhelm the minuses from the stocks that don't work out.

29. Long-term investing has gotten so popular, it's easier to admit you're a crack addict than to admit you're a short-term investor.

30. Visiting stores and testing products is one of the critical elements of the analyst's job.

31. There seems to be an unwritten rule on Wall Street: If you don't understand it, then put your life savings into it. Shun the enterprise around the corner, which can at least be observed, and seek out the one that manufactures an incomprehensible product.

32. The junior high schools and high schools of America have forgotten to teach one of the most important courses of all. Investing.

33. In the long run, it's not just how much money you make that will determine your future prosperity. It's how much of that money you put to work by saving it and investing it.

Business Quotes by Peter Lynch

34. In business, competition is never as healthy as total domination.

35. When you start to confuse Freddie Mac, Sallie Mae, and Fannie Mae with members of your family, and you remember 2,000 stock symbols but forget the children's birthdays, there's a good chance you've become too wrapped up in your work.

36. If you're lucky enough to have been rewarded in life to the degree that I have, there comes a point at which you have to decide whether to become a slave to your net worth by devoting the rest

of your life to increasing it or to let what you've accumulated begin to serve you.

37. Know what you own, and know why you own it.

38. In this business, if you're good, you're right six times out of ten. You're never going to be right nine times out of ten.

39. The typical big winner in the Lynch portfolio generally takes three to ten years to play out.

40. During the Gold Rush, most would-be miners lost money, but people who sold them picks, shovels, tents, and blue jeans (Levi Strauss) made a nice profit.

41. I talk to hundreds of companies a year and spend hour after hour in heady pow-wows with CEOs, financial analysts, and my colleagues in the mutual-fund business, but I stumble onto the big winners in extracurricular situations, the same way you do.

42. Imagine if you borrowed your parents' car without permission and ran it into a tree, how much better you'd feel if you were incorporated.

43. If a picture is worth a thousand words, in business, so is a number.

44. It's human nature to keep doing something as long as it's pleasurable and you can succeed at it, which is why the world population continues to double every 40 years.

45. The person who turns over the most rocks wins the game. And that's always been my philosophy.

46. It would be wonderful if we could avoid the setbacks with timely exits, but nobody has figured out how to predict them.

47. That's not to say there's no such thing as an overvalued market, but there's no point worrying about it.

48. As I look back on it now, it's obvious that studying history and philosophy was much better preparation for the stock market than, say, studying statistics.

49. In our society, it's been the men who've handled most of the finances, and the women who've stood by and watched men botch things up.

50. The natural-born investor is a myth.

51. The simpler it is, the better I like it.

www.ingramcontent.com/pod-product-compliance
Lightning Source LLC
Chambersburg PA
CBHW040854210326
41597CB00029B/4844